HEART AND SCROLL

Heartfelt Stories From The Masters

by
Simcha Raz

Rendered to English by
Rabbi Dov Peretz Elkins

Mazo Publishers

Heart And Scroll: Heartfelt Stories From The Masters

ISBN 978-1-936778-16-4
Large Print Edition

Published by

Mazo Publishers
P.O. Box 10474
Jacksonville, FL 32247 USA

www.mazopublishers.com
Email: mazopublishers@gmail.com
Tel: 1-815-301-3559

Originally published in Hebrew
(Hakhmay Lev) by Simcha Raz

Dedicated to Bubby Hilda
in celebration of her milestone birthday ... by her family
of children, grandchildren, and great-grandchildren.

Contents

Biographical Briefs

Preface

In the course of many generations a host of edifying stories about the spiritual giants of the Jewish People have accumulated. A large number of these contain within them nuggets of ethical teachings and wise insights.

This collection assembles the acumen and vision of a multitude of teachers of our people, in many generations: men of piety, righteousness, unquestionable integrity, high principles and moral values. They cover subjects such as relations between people, between humans and their Maker, and between an individual and his own soul.

It is my hope and prayer that the work of my hands will be acceptable, and that this work will constitute a modest addition to the uplifting sagacity of the Jewish heritage.

Simcha Raz
B"H, Reunited Jerusalem
The 15th of Shevat, 5764

HEART AND SCROLL

Heartfelt Stories From The Masters

Advocacy

Then And Now

A woman came to the Maggid of Kozhnitz and cried before him that her husband hates her. According to him, she is very unattractive.

Perhaps you are truly unattractive? asked the Maggid.

Hearing this the woman wept even more, and said: When my husband stood under the huppah with me at our wedding, he found me very attractive. He gave me many compliments, and told me how beautiful I was. And now, all of a sudden, I've become so unattractive in his eyes?

The Maggid lifted his hands toward heaven and said: Master of the Universe, this woman is right!

Furthermore we also have the same complaint against You. Long ago, when we stood at Mount Sinai and declared, "We will do and we shall obey," You lavished praise on us, and chose us from all other nations. But now – suddenly – we are scorned by You, and You no longer want to look upon us?

Expert In Diamonds

It happened once that Reb Munya Mosinzon, who was known as an important merchant in precious stones and diamonds, and was considered extremely wealthy, was a guest in the home of Rabbi Shmuel Schneerson of Lubavitch.

One day Reb Munya sat with a group of Hasidim, listening to the rabbi. Their discussion dealt with the difficult situation of the Jews in Russia. In the course of conversation the rabbi spoke in praise of the simple folk there. They work hard from morning to evening, in order to eke out a living for themselves and their families – in order not to require, heaven forbid, any help from the kindness of strangers.

Reb Munya interrupted the conversation and spoke with arrogance: I am surprised at the words of the rabbi, that he makes a whole big deal about the simple folk.

Rabbi Shmuel replied in a gentle fashion: These people have many wonderful qualities inside them.

I don't see any fine qualities in them, reacted Reb Munya, waving his hand dismissively.

The rabbi did not reply to him, but the next day he asked him if he brought with him any diamonds.

I have magnificent diamonds, answered Reb Munya with excitement, and immediately began to set up on the rabbi's table an array of beautiful, sparkling diamonds. As he pointed out one shiny stone that was exceptionally prominent among the display of diamonds, he called out with vigor: This stone is truly a wonder of wonders!

I don't see anything special in this stone, noted the rabbi with a smile. In my view it is a small, broken chip of glass.

My master, one must be an expert in order to appreciate properly the quality of a diamond, answered Reb Munya.

Alluding to the conversation that took place between them the day before, the rabbi replied: A simple Jew – he too is a wonder of wonders. But one must be an expert in order to recognize such!

Rabbi Shmuel Schneerson of Lubavitch

1834 – 1882

Rabbi Shmuel Schneerson of Lubavitch was the youngest son of Rabbi Menahem Mendel Schneerson, author of Tzemach Tzedek, and the fourth rebbe of Chabad Hasidim.

Beginning in his younger years he labored intensely to spread Torah observance to the far reaches of Russia, and because of this was sent to jail by the government.

His writings and sermons were published in a series called "Likutay Torah – Torat Shmuel."

And The Wolf Will Dwell With The Lamb

In Noah's Ark, humans and all the animals in the world were gathered. They all lived together in peace, and no one harmed or disturbed another. Therefore, what is so special in the prophecy of the end of days – "And the wolf will dwell with the lamb"? (Isaiah 11:6)

The answer is that they all lived together at the time of the flood, in a time of trouble. It is natural, therefore, that when there is general danger they must all join together peacefully. Even among humans there are different squabbling factions who join together peacefully in a time of danger, and form a united front for the sake of safety and security.

But the prophet is describing the "end of days" – an era of peace and harmony. In other words, the universal cooperation among humans and animals will come about not when there is danger to frighten them – but because of broad-mindedness, elevated consciousness and purity of heart.

Compassion For All

Rabbi Yisrael Salanter was extremely careful to act with compassion in every way.

It happened once that he came into the bet midrash to pray and say kaddish on the occasion of his father's yahrzeit. Among the worshippers was one gentleman who also came to say kaddish. It was the yahrzeit of his daughter.

According to Jewish law, Rabbi Salanter had priority over all others in leading the prayers. He saw that the other man who came to say kaddish was very disappointed that he could not lead the kaddish in memory of his beloved daughter. Therefore Rabbi Salanter deferred the honor in favor of the man who came in memory of his daughter.

The other worshippers began to whisper one to the other: Rabbi Yisrael is belittling the recitation of kaddish in memory of his father on his yahrzeit.

When Rabbi Yisrael heard this he replied: Heaven forbid! The recitation of kaddish is extremely important to me. But the privilege of honoring in this way my beloved father, may his memory be for a blessing, is not as great as caring for a man who came to vent his sorrow. His leading the prayers is worth more than 100 recitations of the kaddish.

Another story about Rabbi Yisrael Salanter describes him as a man who labored constantly over Torah study and proper behavior. He never engaged in idle chatter.

On one occasion his friends saw Rabbi Yisrael standing in the market, chatting about mundane matters with a certain man, and he was laughing and trying to bring humor to him.

The people in the street were amazed, and asked him: Rabbi,

you are a righteous and upright man, your labor is in the Torah, why do we see you standing in the street chatting about small matters with someone you met in the marketplace?

He replied: This gentleman recently underwent a tragedy, and he is shouldering a heavy burden of sorrow. For this reason I found it necessary to fulfill the mitzvah of "gemilut hasadim" (kindness and compassion) to divert his mind from his sorrow and his pain, and help him laugh a bit.

The Sigh of the Poor Worker

A certain scholar and a poor worker lived in the same neighborhood. The scholar was accustomed to arise early and go to the bet midrash to study Torah. He would then pray with deep feeling, return home and have something to eat, and immediately return to his studies in the bet midrash until the afternoon meal. Then he would return to his work for a short while, and return to the bet midrash to study Torah until the afternoon prayers. After the evening prayers he would continue his studies. This was his daily custom.

The poor worker would also arise early and go to the bet midrash. But he did not have much time for study and prayer, since he was rather poor and had to work hard to feed his family.

Once in a while the two neighbors met as they left their homes, or when returning home. At such a time the scholar would look at the poor worker with an angry eye, who was burdened constantly with worries about making a living, and did not have a great deal of time to study Torah or pray properly. The worker sighed and thought to himself: He hurries and I hurry. He hurries to study Torah and to pray – but I run to vain matters.

When they passed away, the two of them appeared before the Heavenly Court – one with Torah and prayer; the other with empty hands.

The defense attorney took all the accumulation of Torah and mitzvot of the scholar and placed them before the judge.

The prosecutor stood up and took his turn: This man does not deserve to be given Heaven, since he was condescending to the poor worker, and even turned an angry eye toward him.

The judge asked the poor worker: What do you have to show for your life?

He sighed and said: I have no Torah or prayer. I was busy making a living, and I had no time for proper prayer.

The Heavenly Court immediately ordered that a scale be brought. They placed the accumulation of Torah and mitzvot on one side, and the angry eye on the other side, and the second side prevailed.

Then they placed all the days and years of the poor worker on one side, which were empty of Torah and prayer, and on the other side they placed the heartfelt sighs that he uttered when he saw his scholarly neighbor occupied with Torah and mitzvot, and the side with the heartfelt sighs prevailed.

Punishment in This World

It happened once that Rabbi Yisrael Meir HaKohen, (known by the title of his most famous book, Hafetz Hayyim), was traveling with a wagon driver. The wagon driver complained to the rabbi: My earnings are meager. Why do I deserve this?

One does not go before God, said the Hafetz Hayyim, trying to calm the man, as a tzaddik would do. Surely you do not follow God in all your ways. You probably do not obey the mitzvot between one person and another. So God punished you, and you are receiving your penalty in this world.

If so, answered the wagon driver, Why did it happen last night that your fur coat was stolen at the Vilna train station?

Because I too am a sinner in financial matters, answered the Hafetz Hayyim in sincerity. I am also a merchant. It happens sometimes that there is a page in a book that I'm selling that is torn, or has some other disfigurement, but the purchasers are embarrassed to tell me. Therefore I received this punishment.

Do Not Separate Yourself from the Community

Rabbi Pinhas of Koretz was admired and beloved by many. Thus they came to him with their questions and requests, and forced him to lose time studying Torah.

The day after Yom Kippur he prayed to the Master of the Universe this prayer: It is well known before You that I do not chase after the community. My only desire is to merit having proper prayer and to study Your Torah in purity and clarity. But the masses line up at my door and mumble to me. Therefore, my Father in Heaven, grant me kindness and remove from me the spirit of graciousness that you bestow upon me, so that I can cling to You alone. It would be better if the throngs would go away from me and hate me rather than bother me with their problems all the time.

A divine voice came down from Heaven and said: Rabbi Pinhas, I have granted your wish.

The next day Rabbi Pinhas stood at his window and looked out, but not one of the passersby even said "Shalom" to him.

Rabbi Pinhas rejoiced and thank the blessed Creator for this gift. They no longer love him and do not stream to mutter their thoughts.

That same day Rabbi Pinhas took a long time in his preparation for prayer, and then went to the small bet midrash to pray. He saw that no one was in the bet midrash, and was very surprised. He waited and waited – and not one person from the regulars in the community came to the bet midrash. Having no choice, he prayed alone.

Rabbi Pinhas was accustomed every day to sit at the desk in the midst of many guests. But today not even one guest showed up. He sat, ate his meal alone, feeling rejected, finished his meal and recited grace after meals.

His wife began to share her sadness with him. She saw that not one person came to share a meal, and the whole day not one foot stepped on their threshold. So she thought there must be a reason. Her heart was heavy, feeling snubbed. She said: Why do people not like me? She felt ostracized by the community. What was her crime, her sin?

Rabbi Pinhas answered her: It seems that it is God's will to remove from me the kindness of the community in order to punish me, since I prayed to God to terminate my gracefulness from their eyes.

The righteous woman heard about her husband's prayer, and said to him: Pinhas, if we are suffering, then do not cancel your will in favor of the will of the community. Be strong and have courage in worshipping God. But Rabbi Pinhas could not conduct himself that way for a long time.

A Jew can study Torah alone, pray by himself, bind his thoughts to the Creator by himself – but he cannot build a sukkah without help from others.

Rabbi Pinhas needed three Jews to help build his sukkah, since he always builds a very large sukkah, where there is room for a minyan of ten guests. But not one person would agree to help him. Rabbi Pinhas struggled, and planned somehow to build the sukkah by himself.

That evening, when he came into the sukkah and sat at the table, and, as is the Jewish custom, invited our father Abraham, the first of the "Ushpizin" (guests), to visit him, Abraham was not willing to enter. He said: I will never enter a sukkah in which not one Jew is willing to be a guest there.

Rabbi Pinhas realized how much wickedness his request brought – to banish his graciousness in the eyes of the community.

He turned before the Blessed Holy One with this prayer: Have mercy on me, my Father in Heaven! Return to me the graciousness that You took away from me, so that many Jews will want to visit my sukkah and will want to come visit me.

Better that I am occupied less with Torah study and prayer – so that I will not be rejected by my brothers and sisters, the family of Israel, the seed of the holy people. Better is idle time spent with the community than arrogance in isolation.

Rabbi Pinhas of Koretz
1728 – 1790

Rabbi Pinhas of Koretz was one of the leading

students of the Baal Shem Tov, the founder of Hasidism. Rabbi Pinhas spread Hasidism throughout the Ukraine. Among his followers were many rabbis and community leaders.

Selections of his teachings were published in these books: "Likutay Shoshanim," and "Midrash Pinhas."

Open The Door Immediately!

Rabbi Issar Zalman Meltzer, Rosh Yeshivah of "Etz Hayyim" in Jerusalem, would open his door by himself for everyone who came to visit him. It happened once, as he was lying in bed, that a knock was heard at the door. It was very late on a rainy night. One of his students went to open the door and asked: Who is there?

Rabbi Issar Zalman called out loudly, On a stormy night after midnight, one asks Who is there? Open the door immediately!

Rabbi Issar Zalman Meltzer
1870 – 1953

Rabbi Issar Zalman Meltzer was one of the leading Jewish scholars in recent generations. He was born in Mir, in White Russia, and from a tender age he was recognized as a budding genius. At age 13, he came to the famous Yeshivah of Volozhin, where outstanding scholars studied, and stood out among them. In 1894, he was appointed Rosh Yeshivah in Slobodka, and after three years he established a very large Yeshivah in Slutzk, which became renowned in the Jewish world.

In 1925, he made aliyah to Eretz Yisrael, and served as Rosh Yeshivah of "Etz Hayyim" – the largest yeshivah in Jerusalem. In addition to his excellence as a Torah scholar, he was known for his deep humility, and for his warm relationship to everyone he met. He served as president of the Council of Leading Torah Sages in the Holy Land, and in this role he made great strides for the Haredi community in the State of Israel.

In 1935, his first book, "Even Ha-Ezel" (a commentary on Maimonides), was published, and to this day nine volumes have appeared in the series.

Do We Have A Choice?

A Russian officer asked the rabbi of Kovno, Rabbi Yitzhak Elhanan Spector: Why do Jews in Russia compete so much with each other – more than others? With with Poles, Ukrainians, Moldavians, etc., each group is occupied in their own work and their own profession, and do not compete with their fellow citizens. But the Jews in Russia are so competitive with each other.

Rabbi Yitzhak Elhanan replied: Look at the animals. The lion does not prey upon another lion, but it does prey upon other animals. So it is with other animals of prey. Furthermore, fish in the sea – the bigger ones swallow up the smaller ones. Why?

Because land animals have the whole world in which to run. They can go wherever they wish – and then they can find their prey among all the other creatures without having to bother their own kind. But fish are locked in the sea, and must confine themselves to the water. So the bigger ones swallow the little ones.

So it is with my people in Russia, concluded Rabbi Yitzhak Elhanan.

All the different nationalities in the country can live anywhere they wish, and they can find their livelihood without bothering their neighbors, people of their own background. But we Jews are forced to live in a closed, tight area, in the Pale of Settlement, as a result of Russian law. Because of this, Jews are forced to compete with their neighbors. The real guilty party is the Russian government!

Rabbi Yitzhak Elhanan Spector
1817 – 1896

Rabbi Yitzhak Elhanan Spector was one of the leading European rabbis of the 19th century, and one of the most important halakhic decisors in his generation. From age 20, he served as rabbi in several congregations in Eastern Europe, and for more than 30 years he served as rabbi of Kovno, the capital of Lithuania.

Beside his greatness as a Torah scholar, he was a community leader and the moving spirit of the Hovevay Zion movement.

The Rabbi Yitzhak Elhanan Seminary in New York is named for him, as is the district of Nahalat Yitzhak in Tel Aviv.

His books on Jewish law are known for their comprehensiveness as well as their depth – such as "Be-er Yitzhak," "Nahal Yitzhak," and "Ayn Yitzhak."

Seeing, But Not Seen

The Hafetz Hayyim once traveled in his wagon in order to give out free copies of his book to whoever wanted one. When the wagon driver passed near a beautiful garden, filled with fruit trees, he stopped, got off and picked some fruit.

The Hafetz Hayyim saw what he was doing and yelled out: They see us, they see us!

The wagon driver was frightened and returned to his seat. But after he calmed down, he looked in all directions, and saw that there was no one around. So he asked the Hafetz Hayyim: Why did you cry out? There's not a soul anywhere near us.

You are wrong, answered the Hafetz Hayyim. Someone sees us, but He sees and is not seen.

Why Did the Rabbi Dance?

A friend of Rabbi Meir Simhah HaKohen of Divinsk told this story: It happened once that he came to visit Rabbi Meir Simhah and saw a very strange sight. The rabbi was dancing in a circle with a husband, his wife, and their child.

The man did not understand, and in his total amazement, he

watched this peculiar sight.

Rabbi Meir Simhah explained to him what happened: The day before, the husband and his wife came to see him in order to receive a "get" (Jewish bill of divorce). The husband presented his complaints, and the wife explained her side. Then Rabbi Meir Simhah asked them: Do you have children?

Yes, we have one son, they answered.

And with whom will the son live after delivery of the "get?" With the mother or with the father? asked Rabbi Meir Simhah, as if talking to himself. He then added immediately, saying to them: Come back tomorrow with the child.

When they returned the next day, with the child, Rabbi Meir Simhah took the child, sat him on his knees and began to cry: My son, said the rabbi, from now on you will be an orphan – with no father and no mother.

The child began to cry too. Then the mother broke out in bitter tears. The father also began to weep.

At that very moment the couple decided not to get divorced, concluded the rabbi, and we all started to dance together from great joy.

Beautiful Before the Sin, and After the Sin

It happened once that Rabbi Aryeh Levin sat with his teacher, the gaon Rabbi Hayyim Berlin, the rabbi of Jerusalem, and read together the biblical book, Song of Songs. When they came to the verse, "You are fair, my darling, you are fair, with your dove-like eyes" (1:15), his teacher's eyes began to weep.

Rabbi Aryeh asked him: Why are you crying? These verses describe how beautiful is the love between the Blessed Holy One and the Jewish people!

Rabbi Hayyim replied with a story: When I served as a rabbi in Moscow, a distinguished man approached me and asked to speak with me alone.

I was recently blessed with a son, he said to me, and I request that you perform "brit milah" (circumcision) for him.

Wonderful! But why such secrecy?

I am a wealthy man, and I sell Christian crosses. But no one knows that I am a Jew. So I want to have the "brit milah" secretly.

At the advice of Rabbi Hayyim, he dismissed all the non-Jewish servants in his house. While Rabbi Hayyim performed the circumcision the father served as Sandek, and the "brit milah" took place in secret, without even the required minyan.

Three days later the father of the baby came to Rabbi Hayyim and placed on his table a sum of money for his effort. But Rabbi Hayyim refused to accept it, and asked: In your house there is no sign of Judaism, and you yourself struggle with all your might to hide the fact that you are a Jew. So why did you want so much to have your son circumcised?

Rabbi, answered the man, I know that I have traveled far from my Jewish faith. I am not even certain that I will ever be able to return and come close to my Maker. It is certain that my baby son will never know what Judaism is. He will not grow up among Jews who have studied the mitzvot, or at least observe the tradition. However, if one day he desires to be a complete Jew, I do not want there to be any obstacle in his path.

Rabbi Hayyim continued: When I read the biblical verse, "You are fair, my darling, you are fair, with your dove-like eyes," I remembered that experience in Moscow, and now I understand why the Bible repeats the words "You are fair." The ancient rabbis taught: "You are fair before you sin, you are fair even after you sin." Why? Since your eyes are like doves. And further, it is taught in the Talmudic tractate Bava Batra (chapter two): "The dove, even when she is far from her home, tries not to be so far that she cannot see the dovecote."

This is what is meant when we read that the Jewish people are beautiful before they sin, and also beautiful after they sin.

A Blessing Before Death

Major General Dany Matt told this story: I was the officer in charge in the Crimea. Several soldiers died, among whom were some who were only children to their parents. I received one letter from the parents of one of these fallen soldiers.

It was a very unusual letter, full of complaints about the Israeli Army and the State of Israel. At the end of the letter, the father wrote: I wish for you and your family that fate will take revenge on you, and that you will suffer the rest of your life as I am suffering at this moment.

One evening, as I was standing at the Western Wall, Simhah Holtzberg, well known as "the father of the wounded," approached me, and suggested that I visit the tzaddik Rabbi Aryeh Levin. We went together. This was a few months before Rabbi Aryeh's death, and he was already confined to his sickbed.

Simhah Holtzberg presented me to him, and told Rabbi Aryeh about the awful letter that I had received from the bereaved father, which contained the terrible curse. He then asked Rabbi Aryeh, Please give him a blessing! After receiving such a letter it is most fitting that you bless him. Rabbi Aryeh took my hand, placed it between his two palms, and blessed me. I don't remember exactly what he said – but I felt like a small child.

A short time later Simhah Holtzberg told me that Rabbi Aryeh was mortally ill, and was taken to the hospital. When we arrived at Hadassah Hospital, the corridor was filled with Jews praying for his welfare. When we entered his room, we saw an unusual sight: Rabbi Aryeh was not in his bed, but resting in a lounge chair, folded over into himself.

Simhah touched Rabbi Aryeh several times with a light nudge, and said to him: Rabbi Aryeh, do you know who is here? The captain from Gush Etzion who was with you.

Suddenly Rabbi Aryeh stirred and mumbled: Is that the captain with the missing finger? Simhah answered, "Yes," and Rabbi Aryeh grabbed my hand and squeezed it. Before I could pull it back, he kissed my hand, and said to Simhah: My tallit katan is over there in the corner. Would you please wrap it around my shoulder. Then he blessed my wife, my children, and me. The hour was almost seven in the evening.

That night Rabbi Aryeh breathed his last breath in purity.

Why Pronounce a Curse When a Blessing is Better?

A Jewish tourist from America wanted to put an end to Israel's troubles. What did he do? He went to visit the tzaddik Rabbi Aryeh Levin, and suggested that he curse Nasser, the president of Egypt, that he drop dead.

I, answered Rabbi Aryeh, never cursed anyone in my entire life. This is the vocation of Balaam the evil one. I would rather bless Nasser that he merit to see the coming of the Messiah. And if he merits this, we will no longer need curses.

Too Late Now

A certain student was diagnosed with a sickness that threatened his life, Heaven forbid. He visited his teacher, the Hafetz Hayyim, in Radin, to request a blessing, since the doctors already told him that his case is hopeless. Every day that passed, his family lost more hope.

The Hafetz Hayyim listened to the young student, and told him that he would give him some advice – but only on condition that he never tell anyone. The student immediately agreed.

The Hafetz Hayyim directed him to go to a certain scholar

who lives in a small village.

Tell him about your situation, said the Hafetz Hayyim, and request a blessing from him. He will grant you a blessing, and with God's help you will be cured.

The young man listened to his teacher, went right away to the scholar, and received a blessing. Lo and behold, soon after, in a miraculous way, he was cured. He continued to study in the yeshivah, and after a while he left Radin and raised a family. Just as he had been asked, he never told anyone about the mysterious events.

More than twenty years passed, and the sister-in-law of the student came down with a mysterious disease. Very soon it became clear that she was suffering from the same illness that he had had before. Every time she spoke about it, he changed the subject. However, his wife and his sister-in-law pleaded with him to reveal what happened to him, and how he was cured, in the hope that his secret would help save the patient. Finally his resistance weakened, and he told the details of the cure from his serious illness. His wife and sister-in-law were filled with hope. Perhaps she too will be cured.

Soon after, the man began to feel bad. He was frightened, and decided to travel to Radin to the Hafetz Hayyim, who was then elderly and weak. The Hafetz Hayyim remembered their first meeting. He listened carefully in silence to the man's story, and then spoke very softly and slowly.

I wish I could help you! But what can I do now? When the disease afflicted you before, I was young, and I fasted forty days for your sake, in order that you be cured. But today I am already old, and I cannot fast as I did then.

Burying the Dead

The Grave of a Groom Next to the Grave of His Father-in-Law

The holy tzaddik of Jerusalem, Rabbi Aryeh Levin, told this story: One evening I went from Meah Shearim to my home in the neighborhood of Mish'kenot Yisrael. When I passed by the old Hadassah Hospital, I noticed the room where cadavers were kept. I heard a crying voice coming from the room. I went in and saw an elderly woman and three young women, apparently her daughters, standing and crying over a deceased person.

I noticed that the family was alone, with no one to share their sorrow. I could not leave them, crying by themselves.

Suddenly I heard the woman cry out: Your holy ancestors will come to welcome you!

I was very curious about the matter, so I approached the woman and asked her who his ancestors were.

The woman answered amidst despair: And if I tell you, will you recognize them?

I persisted and replied: Nevertheless… Perhaps…

The woman relented and told me that his grandfather was Rabbi Alinka of Ledah. Rabbi Alinka of Ledah? Rabbi Eliyahu Shik of Ledah was his grandfather? Therefore, who was his father? Perhaps Rabbi Pinyeleh?

The woman was amazed. Oh God in heaven, how do you know all this? Yes, Rabbi Pinyeleh, the son of Rabbi Alinka of Ledah was my husband's father. My husband, Rabbi Moshe Aharon, was a well-known teacher from Odessa. But here no one knows us.

Of course I immediately did everything in my power to arrange for a proper burial for this honorable gentleman. I went out into the street, and assembled anyone I knew, and I assembled a small group. I arranged to have the finest shroud, and some beautiful words of eulogy were recited. We accompanied the deceased to the cemetery, and afterwards I arranged to have visitors come to comfort the widow and her daughters.

After some months I received a letter from Hadera, from the family of the deceased. In the letter there was an invitation to a wedding. One of the three daughters was getting married. I could not attend, even though I had wanted to very much.

Another few months passed, and a young man came to see me. He told that that he was the groom of the family from Hadera who were well known to me, and that he was seeking employment. I received him graciously, and asked him to visit me again if he remained in Jerusalem. He promised to visit me again.

However, about a week later I was called to Hadassah Hospital. I went quickly to the hospital and found the young man lying there, mortally ill, after a serious operation.

I discovered that he had first come to Jerusalem for an operation, but he did not want to trouble me. Thus he pretended that he was coming to find work. In the hospital he gave my name as one who was close to him, to whom they should turn in an emergency.

The young man suffered much pain for several days, and finally expired. During these few days I came to recognize that he was a young man of fine character and an observant Jew. Even the nurses in the hospital, and all those who had contact with him had only praiseworthy things to say about him.

The added tragedy for this family moved me greatly, and I was very depressed. I participated in the funeral, which took place late in the evening.

All this took place in Eretz Yisrael in a time of great tumult. Going to the Mount of Olives was very dangerous. Therefore armed guards accompanied every funeral.

Just before the funeral procession proceeded to the cemetery, I approached the head of the Hevrah Kadisha, and told him that I was acquainted with the deceased young man. I told him that he was a God-fearing Jew. And that I knew his father-in-law, who was a well-known and distinguished rabbi. And that his father-in-law was buried on the Mount of Olives, in the newer section of the cemetery. Next to his grave there is surely some open land, and that it would be most fitting for the young man to be buried next to his father-in-law, since this is ancestral burial ground.

The head of the Hevrah Kadisha looked at me in great anger.

I am amazed at you, he said. You know that this is a very dangerous time. Two armed guards are accompanying us, and we are jeopardizing ourselves by going at this late hour to the Mount of Olives. We will hurry to go there to complete our work as quickly as possible. We will go to the first open grave we find, bury the dead, and rush back to the city. Do you think it wise at this hour to search for other graves, and add more danger to our lives?

I bowed my head in shame after listening to these words, since I knew he was right. I hurried to add: You are right. I did not realize the reality of this situation. Now that I am aware, I will not ask anything else.

The funeral procession continued on its way.

As the leader requested, so it was. Everything was accomplished quickly, with fear of great danger. We all took the deceased to the new section of the cemetery, and at the first open plot we brought the body for burial.

In order to properly mark the place of the grave, the leader placed a stone that was leaning on the adjoining grave, which did not have a tombstone. On this stone, on its other side, was written the name of the person buried there – "Rabbi Moshe Aharon ben Pinhas Shick."

When I read this name, my entire body shook. I returned to the head of the Hevrah Kadisha and asked him with a shaking voice: Do you know who is buried here – in the next grave? This is the father-in-law of the deceased! It was next to this man that I wanted to bury the body!

The leader reacted in amazement: What can we possibly say? Something like this has never happened to me in my entire life!

Circumcision

A Tzaddik Escapes from Trouble

This is a story about a pious Jew, a man who was honorable and upright, a lover of mitzvot and acts of kindness. He was a "mohel" (circumciser of babies), who loved to perform this mitzvah.

This pious Jew was the official treasurer of the king, and knew all his secrets. The king always followed his advice, since he was faithful and honest in all matters.

Another court official was jealous of the treasurer and tried to harm him. This pious Jew had a faithful servant. The evil court official gave the treasurer's servant a bribe, so that he could steal from his pious master the key to the chest in which all the king's secret letters were locked up. The servant gave the evil court official the key, and he a stole a large package, full of secret papers and letters.

One day, when the evil official was with the king, he mentioned a certain secret that he had stolen from the king's chest. The king was aghast that this official knew of the secret matter, and the official told the king that the pious Jew was the one who told it to him.

The king grew angry that the Jew revealed his secret, and decided to have him killed – but he decided to do it in secret.

So the king called the pious Jew and handed him a letter to one of his generals who lived very far from the palace – a distance of eight hours. In that place was a fortress to which the king sent all the people that he wanted to kill away from the public eye.

The king wrote a letter to the general: When you read this letter, immediately have the man who carries it killed, and pay no attention to any claims he may present to you about his innocence.

The king sealed the letter, handed it to the pious Jew, and told him: This is a secret letter that I wrote to the general of the fortress, and I am trusting only you to give it to him.

The pious Jew immediately climbed on to his wagon, together with his faithful servant, and off they went to find the general. While still on the road, they met one of the people from a nearby town, who requested that he go to his home and circumcise his son, born exactly eight days before.

In his great enthusiasm to be honored to perform the mitzvah, he consented to do the "brit milah" (circumcision). So he gave the letter to his servant, and instructed him to deliver the letter to the hand of the general and to wait there until he himself arrived. Meanwhile he went with the father, fulfilled the mitzvah of "brit milah," and remained with them for the evening to attend the festive mitzvah meal.

At midnight, after the meal, the pious Jew resumed his wagon trip to the general to meet up with his servant.

Early the next morning the pious Jew arrived at the fortress. The general saw the wagon in the distance, and immediately identified him as an officer of the king. So he left his fortress to greet him, met the well-known pious man, and asked him: Why, sir, did you bother yourself to come here? Did you think that I would not fulfill the wish of the king? Did I not, as soon as the servant handed me the letter, grab him and kill him, according to the command of the king in his letter? And I did not give any credence to the claims that he presented to save himself – since that was the order of the king in his letter.

The pious Jew understood that he was saved from the terrible fate that was waiting for him.

The general continued: My lord, it is really a good thing that you came here, since before the servant was taken out to die he recited a confession that justified the order – that he had indeed sinned and disobeyed you. He stole the key to the king's chest of secret letters, and that is how they came to the hands of the evil officer. The pious Jew was terribly disturbed to hear the story told him by the general, and so he returned to the palace and approached the king.

When the king saw him, he was shocked, and asked him: Where have you come from? Did you not give the letter to the general as I told you?

The pious Jew related to the king everything that happened, and even suggested that he send his police to the home of the evil officer, where he would find the secret letters that were stolen from him.

The king did as was suggested, and indeed the letters were found. Immediately they caught the evil officer and brought him to the king with the letters. The king decreed to have him killed for his disobedience, and he admired and loved the pious Jew even more than before, and promoted him.

The words of the Bible were fulfilled for the pious Jew: "The righteous person is rescued from trouble, and the wicked one takes his place" (Proverbs 11:8).

The Power of Tears

It happened once that a very sad woman went to visit Rabbi Aryeh Levin, and asked if she could sit with him a while to cry her heart out.

You can sit, of course, said Rabbi Aryeh. But crying – you have to cry before the Blessed Holy One, not to me. God hears the sound of crying, and listens to the anguish of His children.

The woman sat across from him, and cried and cried and cried. She told him all the troubles her husband was having. He was mortally ill.

Don't cry, said the rabbi. God will have pity and heal him.

Several days later he heard that her husband had died. Rabbi Aryeh went to comfort her, and found her crying bitterly. Rabbi Aryeh comforted her and encouraged her with words that entered her heart.

I will be comforted, she said to him, as long as you can tell me what happened to the torrent of my tears, tears with which I moistened the Book of Psalms in my hand, all the days that I cried before the Blessed Holy One during the time my late husband was ill.

Rabbi Aryeh replied: In 120 years from now, when you stand before the heavenly court, you will find out how many harsh decrees on our people were cancelled due to the pure tears that poured from your eyes.

No tears are lost, Rabbi Aryeh continued. The Blessed Holy One counts every tear and collects them in His precious storehouse of tears.

Again the woman burst out in tears, but this time in tears of joy.

After some time the widow returned to Rabbi Aryeh's home and said: Rabbi, tell me again the same beautiful words. What was the fate of my many tears?

Two Chosen Mountains

Rabbi Hayyim of Tzanz used to say: There are two chosen mountains: Mount Sinai – on which the Torah was given to the Jewish people; and Mount Moriah – on which our father Abraham bound his son Yitzhak, and on which the Holy Temple was built.

Is it not puzzling: Why was the Holy Temple not built on Mount Sinai, which was sanctified by the giving of the Torah?

The answer is that a place on which a Jew showed such dedication, and was ready to lay his neck on the altar to be sacrificed – that is sanctified to God more than the place where the Holy Presence, the Shekhinah, was revealed, and the Torah was given.

Reducing the Suffering

Rabbi Levi Yitzhak of Berditchev would visit every sick person in his city. It happened once that he visited a sick person and found him suffering.

Rabbi Levi Yitzhak asked him: What are you worried about?

The man replied: Rabbi, I am worried that my days are numbered. My heart is full of anxiety. What will be my portion in the world to come?

Rabbi Levi Yitzhak told him: I am giving you as a gift my entire share in the world to come.

The face of the sick man suddenly turned happy, but shortly thereafter he died.

One of the friends of Rabbi Levi Yitzhak said to him: Rabbi, surely your intention was to keep the sick man alive for some time. But now you see that this was his last hour, and your encouragement did not help him at all. What was the use of all this?

Listen, my son, said Rabbi Levi Yitzhak, I am ready to contribute my place in the world to come, even in order to save one minute of pain from a Jew who is mortally ill.

Rabbi Levi Yitzhak of Berditchev
1740 – 1809

Rabbi Levi Yitzhak of Berditchev was a teacher and master to many. He was born to a family of rabbis of substantial lineage in Galicia.

When he relocated to Poland he was influenced by Hasidism and became a student of Rabbi Dov Ber, the Maggid of Mezritch. After serving in several communities, at age 45 he settled in Berditchev, where he served as rabbi and leader until his death.

He was active in the community, but his major energy was devoted to establishing Hasidism in the center of Poland, in Lithuania and in the Ukraine. He traveled frequently and educated large masses of people in the worship of God with joy and enthusiasm.

Rabbi Levi Yitzhak became known for his love of the Jewish people. He did not miss an opportunity to defend his people. He believed that even when Jews are involved in the most earthly, material matters, they never stop worshipping God.

His sermons were collected in "Kedushat Levi."

One God and Two Worlds

When Rabbi Yosef Yitzhak of Lubavitch was investigated by the Russian secret police, he refused to stop his activities in strengthening Jewish life.

One of the investigators threatened him with a gun and said: This little "toy" has changed the minds of many people...

The master was not afraid and answered calmly: This small toy can frighten one who believes in many gods and one world. However I have one God and two worlds (this world and the world to come), and this toy doesn't scare me at all!

Rabbi Yosef Yitzhak Schneerson of Lubavitch
1880 – 1950

Rabbi Yosef Yitzhak Schneerson was the grandson of Rabbi Shmuel of Lubavitch. From his youth he fought with great dedication for the spread of Torah in all corners of Russia. He was imprisoned for his actions, but later miraculously freed.

For a while he lived in Riga, the capital of Latvia, and in Warsaw, the capital of Poland.

The last ten years of his life Rabbi Yosef Yitzhak lived in New York, and was extremely successful in spreading Torah and Judaism throughout American Jewry.

His many lectures and essays were published in "Sefer HaMa-amarim," "Sifray HaSihot," and in "Likutay Dibburim."

God Loves All His Creatures

In the days of the British Mandate in the Holy Land, the British rulers turned to the Chief Rabbi, Rabbi Yitzhak Isaac HaLevi Herzog, and asked him to invite the tzaddik Rabbi Aryeh Levin, who visited Jewish underground fighters, to also visit Arab prisoners. It was well known that Rabbi Aryeh had a special way, with his warm face and sparkling eyes, in giving comfort and relief to those in need.

Rabbi Herzog requested that Rabbi Aryeh fulfill this mitzvah, and he readily and willingly agreed, saying, "Beloved are all people who are created in the image of God."

Rabbi Yitzhak Isaac HaLevi Herzog
1888 – 1959

Rabbi Yitzhak Isaac HaLevi Herzog was the first Ashkenazic Chief Rabbi of the State of Israel. He was born in Lomza, Poland, and received his doctoral degree from the University of London for his thesis on the color of the tassels of the tallit in ancient times.

He served as rabbi of the Jewish community of Belfast in Northern Ireland and in Dublin. In 1921, he was appointed Chief Rabbi of Ireland. In 1936, he was invited to make aliyah to Eretz Yisrael to inherit the position of Chief Rabbi Avraham Yitzhak Kook. In 1937, he became Chief Ashkenazi Rabbi of Eretz Yisrael. After World War II, he made great efforts to save the Jewish refugees and orphans in Europe.

His oldest son, Chaim Herzog, became the sixth President of the State of Israel.

Encouragement Even After Death

A woman lost her only son who was killed in the war of "Peace of the Galilee." From the time of his death, she lost all zest for life and any desire to continue living. She stayed home all the time.

It happened that she attended a funeral of a pious woman who was one of her close friends. The funeral procession was scheduled to leave from the cemetery in the area of Sanhedria. Since she was a bit early to the funeral, she decided to visit the grave of the tzaddik Rabbi Aryeh Levin, which was nearby, and recite some chapters of the Book of Psalms. She thought that perhaps the merit of the tzaddik would stand her in good stead, and help heal her pain.

At the grave of Rabbi Aryeh she saw written on his tombstone: "I request that all who come to prostrate themselves on my grave recite these words with a full heart: 'I believe with perfect faith that there will be resurrection of the dead at an appropriate hour, when the blessed Creator so desires.'"

The woman was deeply moved and she began to mumble to

herself: What? There will be resurrection of the dead? Therefore surely I will merit to see again my only son who fell in the war.

From that time on the woman was encouraged, and her desire returned to continue living, believing and hoping. Thus the famous tzaddik, Rabbi Aryeh Levin, merited to bestow kindness on a bereaved mother and encouraged her even after his death.

Eretz Yisrael

The Healing Air of Eretz Yisrael

An American Jew who decided to make aliyah, under the influence of the Chief Rabbi, Avraham Yitzhak HaKohen Kook, suddenly had regret and decided to return to the Diaspora. Before his departure he visited Rabbi Kook to ask for his blessing.

Why are you leaving, so suddenly? asked the rabbi.

Life here in Eretz Yisrael has disappointed me. I cannot tolerate the religious chaos that has spread among the pioneers and the settlements. So I decided to leave and return to America.

Rabbi Kook hesitated for a moment, and then asked his guest where he lived in America.

I live in Denver, Colorado, he answered. With great pride and patriotism the man began to describe Denver and its beauty. It has clean, pure air, and has no narrow, dirty alleyways – he continued mockingly – as there are here in Jerusalem. He continued to praise the beauty of nature which surrounds Denver.

Rabbi Kook interrupted him. It seems to me, he said, that in the city of Denver there are many sick people with chronic disease, with no hope of a cure. If the climate of Denver is so healthy and healing, why are there so many sick people there?

The people there, answered the man, are not natives. They come there from other cities which have no fresh air or sunlight. In their hometowns they became ill, and on the advice of their physicians they come to Denver to enjoy the pure, healing air.

The rabbi interrupted and said to him gently: Do your ears hear what your lips are saying? That's exactly how our healing, Holy Land helps so many people.

Unfortunate Jews come here from all the lands of the Diaspora, where the atmosphere influences their soul, and makes them spiritually ill. Their destiny, Heaven forbid, would be to assimilate among the nations, and to die a spiritual death on foreign soil.

So if you see people who are spiritually deprived in our Holy Land – these are foreigners, who come to the Holy Land to be healed from their illness through the special, sacred air of Eretz Yisrael.

Those Who Honor Shabbat and Those Who Desecrate Shabbat

A group of important Hasidim approached Rabbi Avraham Yitzhak HaKohen Kook, and complained: Lately the number of those who desecrate Shabbat in the cities of Eretz Yisrael is growing. And the number of those who honor Shabbat is falling below the number of the lands of the Diaspora.

Rabbi Kook answered in his usual gentle manner: Is it not interesting how beloved is the Holy Land compared to the rest of the places in the world?

In the lands of the Diaspora there are even those who observe Shabbat. But in Eretz Yisrael, they say that there are even those who desecrate the Shabbat.

The Beginning of the Jewish Settlement in Eretz Yisrael: In the Graves

A certain active Zionist spoke disparagingly about the older settlement – the Jews who came to Eretz Yisrael to die and be buried in the Holy Land.

Rabbi Kook addressed himself to this issue as follows: The very first purchase of land in Eretz Yisrael began with Abraham, when he asked Efron the Hittite, "Sell me a burial site" (Genesis 23:4). In addition, when the Israelite people left Egypt, they took with them Joseph's bones for burial in the Land. It was from these graves, of our patriarchs, and by their merit, that Eretz Yisrael remained a living land.

Rabbi Avraham Yitzhak HaKohen Kook
1865 - 1935

Rabbi Avraham Yitzhak HaKohen Kook was one of the great rabbis and scholars of recent generations, and Chief Rabbi of Eretz Yisrael from 1921 to 1935.

In his younger years, Rabbi Kook served in several communities in Lithuania. In 1904, he settled in Eretz Yisrael and was appointed Chief Rabbi of Jaffa. In 1919, he was appointed Chief Rabbi of Jerusalem. Two years later he was appointed Chief Ashkenazic Rabbi of Eretz Yisrael, and served in that role until his death.

Rabbi Kook was active in engaging the hearts of many

different groups in the "Yishuv" (Jewish settlement of Eretz Yisrael), especially demonstrating sympathy with, and understanding of the "halutzim" (pioneers) in the moshavim and kibbutzim. In Jerusalem he founded the well-known "Mercaz HaRav," in which hundreds of young men from Eretz Yisrael and the Diaspora studied.

He wrote many books on Jewish law and lore, and on biblical commentaries and Jewish philosophy. The moshav Kfar HaRo-eh is named for him (an acronymn of HaRav Avraham HaKohen Kook). Also carrying his name is Mosad HaRav Kook, which publishes many important Hebrew books.

For the Sake of Settling the Land of Israel

It happened once that Rabbi Shmuel Mohliver came to one of the larger cities in Russia to promote settlement in Eretz Yisrael. The rabbis of the city, and all its significant leaders, came to honor Rabbi Shmuel. The rabbi lectured to the large throng about the importance of the mitzvah of building the Land. It is, he said, equal to all the other mitzvot in the Torah, and he requested a contribution for that cause.

One of the people at the meeting, a learned and observant Jew arose and said: Our teacher, I am prepared to make a generous contribution for the settlement of Eretz Yisrael, but there are many who oppose this idea. Some say this is forcing God's hand.

Others argue that almost all those working for settlement in the Land are not God-fearing Jews. Because of this I, along with others, am reluctant to support them.

Rabbi Shmuel replied: I will tell you a true story. In one of the small towns there lived a young man who was diligent in Torah study. His father, who was not at all wealthy, sent him from time to time a sum of money, addressed to the "shohet" (ritual slaughterer) of the town. Each time the son would confirm receipt of the money.

It happened once that the young man received a letter from his father in which he wrote that several months before he had sent him 25 rubles, addressed to the shohet. But this time he did not receive confirmation that it was received. The young man was amazed, since it had been a long time since he had received a penny from the shohet. The young man therefore went to the shohet to clarify the matter, and the shohet declared that he had not received the 25 rubles.

The matter was discussed over and over. The father wrote that he had sent the money, and the shohet argued that he had not received it.

The young man called the shohet to a Din Torah, and it was decided that the shohet was obliged to take an oath. The shohet removed from his pocket 25 rubles in order to give it to the young man, and at the same time swore that the money never reached him.

The rabbi and those nearby were surprised and said to the shohet: If you paid him, why did you swear? And if you swore, what did you pay?

The shohet replied: If I had only sworn and had not paid, some would suspect that I had really received the money, and my oath was false. And if I had only paid the money and not sworn, they would suspect that certainly I received the money, and only because I was afraid to swear I changed my mind and returned the stolen money. But now that I have both sworn and paid the money, everyone sees that I did not touch money that was not mine, and that my oath was honest.

Rabbi Shmuel concluded: So it is in the matter of settling the Land. Those who pretend to be God-fearing but come with complaints about the settlement – let them first make a contribution – and afterwards they can come and complain. Then everyone will believe that their complaint is sincere, and what is in their heart is on their tongue. But if they come with a complaint, but do not contribute – there is room to suspect that all their complaints are only to release them from a contribution.

Rabbi Shmuel Mohliver
1824 – 1898

Shmuel Mohliver was a pioneer of religious zionism. In 1882, he met with Baron Rothschild in Paris and influenced him to support the Jews who were rebuilding Israel.

Mohliver was appointed Rabbi of Bialystok in 1883 and convinced Bialystok's Jews to move to Petah Tikva, then a small settlement in Israel.

In Mohliver's last letter to the Jews of Russia before his death, he urged them to work to achieve a deep attachment to the commandment to settle in Israel, which he said is "the foundation of the existence of our people."

People with Elevated Souls

A Chabad Hasid from Eretz Yisrael once came to Lubavitch to visit the son of the Rebbe, who was his relative.

The Rebbe inquired as to the welfare of the Jews in Eretz Yisrael, and he replied: I don't understand what is written in books – that in Eretz Yisrael live people with elevated souls. I know Jews in Eretz Yisrael, but I have not found among them with souls elevated higher than those in the Diaspora.

The Rebbe asked: Do you know what a Jew with an elevated soul is? Let me tell you a story that I heard from my father, of blessed memory, and you will see how high sometimes the power of a simple Jew in Eretz Yisrael can be.

In a small village near Jerusalem lived a simple Jew. He did not study Torah, and he did not even understand the meaning of the words in the prayers. Not only that, but he did not know the order of the prayers – namely, what someone recites on each day. Each week he would come to Jerusalem and visit one of the rabbis, and he would write down for him what to pray on each day during the coming week.

It happened once, during the month of Heshvan, that he came to Jerusalem, and to his surprise he saw that all the Jewish shops were closed. The Jew was frightened – perhaps he made a mistake, and today was in fact Shabbat. He noticed a Jew walking in the street wearing tallit and tefillin, and he felt better. It is not Shabbat today, since on Shabbat we don't wear tefillin. He then asked the Jew why all the shops were closed. The man replied that today was a public fast day.

The villager was surprised that his rabbi did not write down for him the occurrence of this fast day, and he was sorry that he made two mistakes: that he ate on a fast day, and that he did not pray as one should on a public fast day.

He ran to his rabbi, and found him in the synagogue. He asked him why he did not tell him about the proper rules for this fast day.

His rabbi explained: Relax, my son, this is not a fixed fast day. Rather it is a special fast for rain that we decreed in Jerusalem.

And what is that, asked the Jew, a fast for rain?

His rabbi explained: If there is no rain, and there is danger of a drought, we decree a fast and pray to God that rain will fall.

The Jew was surprised. For this, one decrees a fast?

Why not, asked the rabbi. What else, in your opinion, is there to do?

The Jew replied: When there is no rain on my field, I go out to the field and cry out to God: Father, I need rain! Immediately the rain begins to fall.

So, my son, why not do this here?

The villager went out to the courtyard of the synagogue, and began to cry out: Father! Is it possible that your children in the Holy City will die, God forbid, from hunger? Don't you see that they need rain? Immediately rains of blessing began to fall.

When the Rebbe finished his story to the visitor from Eretz Yisrael, he said to him: Do you now appreciate who in Eretz Yisrael has an elevated soul?

Rabbi Menahem Mendel Schneerson
1789 – 1866

Rabbi Menahem Mendel Schneerson of Lubavitch

was appointed in 1827 as the third leader of Chabad Hasidim. For 40 years he successfully led thousands of Hasidim. Like the Chabad rebbes who preceded him, he founded in Russia several agricultural settlements for the sustenance of his followers.

He was a giant in Torah and a prolific author in all fields of Jewish studies. He is called the Tzemah Tzedek, as this is the title of his book containing many halakhic responsa, and novella on Torah and commentaries that he wrote on tractates of the Talmud.

Many of Rabbi Schneerson's sermons on the Tanakh were published in a series of books called Or HaTorah. However many of his writings have still not been published. In his book "Derekh Mitzvotekha," he explains in detail the reasons for the mitzvot.

Two People Seeing Differently

Two tourists went to tour a big city and see what it's like. When they returned they were asked about their impressions.

One said: I roamed around the entire city, and I found it full of wise men, authors, fine merchants and knowledgeable leaders. The city is filled with beautiful synagogues and schools. Large throngs of citizens visit these places and study Torah diligently. There are even people who are so committed that they study day and night.

The other visitor reacted thus: I found that the residents are lazy, do-nothings, and many are evil sinners.

The listeners were astonished. How is such a thing possible? Which of the two is telling the truth, and which is just lying?

In the crowd stood a wise man, and explained to the listeners: Each of them saw what their heart wanted to see, and told only half the truth. They each reflected their own personality. One had a dark attitude, and saw only darkness. The other was a happy and positive person, and he saw what was positive.

It's not the world you see, but how you see the world!

Forbidden to Speak Ill of Eretz Yisrael

An emissary from Eretz Yisrael arrived in Volozhin, where Rabbi Naftali Tzvi Yehudah Berlin lived (the Netziv of Volozhin). The Gaon received the emissary graciously, prepared for him a table filled with fine foods, and spent a long hour serving him food and drink. All the while he spoke emotionally, saying, My dear guest! Guest from our Holy Land!

After the meal the Netziv inquired about what is happening in the Holy Land, both physically and spiritually. The guest sighed heavily, and began to tell about the spiritual deterioration of the new generation compared to their parents.

In anger, the Netziv arose from his seat and shouted to his guest: I refuse to hear bad tidings about our Holy Land. Speak no more!

Believe me, my master, answered the emissary defensively, I am telling the truth, and do not swerve an inch from the truth.

If so, said the Netziv in anger, you are acting just like the spies in the desert. They too told the people the truth, as they saw it with their own eyes during the forty days that they toured the Land. Nevertheless they were punished for their words with the full measure of the law, as it is written: "Those who spread such calumnies about the Land died by the plague, by the will of the Lord" (Numbers 14:37).

Rabbi Naftali Tzvi Yehudah Berlin of Volozhin
1817 – 1893

Rabbi Naftali Tzvi Yehudah Berlin (HaNetziv) was one of the great scholars of the second half of the 19th century. He was born in Mir in the district of Minsk, the capital of White Russia, and in his youth became known as a prodigy.

In 1853 he was appointed Rosh Yeshiva of Volozhin, and served in that role for 40 years – until the yeshivah was closed by the Russian government in 1892. He was an exceptional educator, and had thousands of students from many communities. In his day the Yeshivah of Volozhin became the spiritual center of Eastern European Jewry. One of his sons, Rabbi Meir Berlin, served for many years as head of Mizrahi, the religious Zionist movement.

Among his books are "Mayshiv Davar" (halakhic responsa) and "Ha-amek Davar" (biblical commentary). The kibbutz "Ayn HaNetziv" in the Bet Shean valley is named after him.

First Yitgadal, and afterward, Yitkadash

Rabbi Meir Simhah of Divinsk was an enthusiastic supporter of the settlement of Eretz Yisrael, and rejoiced every time a new moshav was built.

Rabbi, asked one of his friends one day, What good is the settlement of the Land, if it is done by secular Zionists, who do not follow the ways of Torah and mitzvot?

The rabbi replied: In the Kaddish prayer, we say "Yitgadal ve-yitkadash sh'may rabba." First we say Yitgadal, "May God's name be great, and only after that do we naturally add Yitkadash, "May God's name be sanctified."

Rabbi Meir Simhah HaKohen of Divinsk
1843 – 1926

Rabbi Meir Simhah HaKohen of Divinsk was one of the giants of the late 19th and early 20th century. Until age 45 he lived in Bialystok, where he lived and studied with his father-in-law. His reputation as a great Torah scholar grew and grew. Still, he declined to accept a rabbinic position for many years.

In 1888, he commenced serving as a teacher in Divinsk, in White Russia, along with the great rabbinic scholar Rabbi Yosef Rosen, the Rogatchover. Due to these scholars Divinsk served as the leading Torah center for many decades.

His major works include "Meshekh Hokhmah," and "Or Sameah."

The Evil Inclination

To What Does the Evil Inclination Resemble?

Rabbi Nahman of Breslov taught this lesson: The Evil Inclination resembles a person who is running down the street with his fist closed, and no one knows what is in his hand. Everyone thinks to himself that what is in that clenched fist is something he wants. So everyone chases after him. But when the man stops for a second, and opens his hand, it becomes clear that his hand is empty.

It's the same way with the Evil Inclination. It deceives the whole world, and everyone runs after it, because they mistakenly think that what is inside of it is something they desperately want. In the end, when the Evil Inclination opens his hand, they all see that there is nothing there.

Rabbi Nahman explained further. All the desires of this world resemble a pillar of light, which penetrates into the home from the light of the sun. People want to capture the pillar of light, but they cannot – since it exists only from the strength of the shining of the sun. So it is with the pillar of human desire. The desires of this world cannot be captured in one's hand.

Rabbi Nahman of Breslov
1772 – 1810

Rabbi Nahman of Breslov was the great grandson of the Baal Shem Tov, and like his great grandfather, he was a sensitive soul who often indulged in seclusion and self-mortification.

In 1798, he made aliyah to Eretz Yisrael. His residence in the Holy Land brought him great spiritual elevation, however for whatever reason he returned to Breslov. At the end of his life he settled in Uman, in the Ukraine.

Rabbi Nahman told many stories and led many discussions, which were compiled by his students in several books, including "Likutay Maharan," "Likutay Halakhot," "Sefer HaMidot," "Sippuray Maasiyot," and "Likutay Tefillot."

The Pretensions of the Evil Inclination

One wintry day, after morning prayers, Rabbi Pinhas of Koretz sat in the bet midrash and heard a discussion of Hasidim about the wiles of the "Yetzer HaRa" (Evil Inclination), which uses all kinds of tricks to capture people into its lair and seduce them to sin.

Rabbi Pinhas taught them: I hate the Evil Inclination not because it instigates and seduces, but because it deceives and fools people. Never have I heard that the Evil Inclination comes to a Jew and says to him: Commit such and such a sin. Rather when it wants to seduce someone away from the proper path, it comes and pretends to be righteous, and says: Do such and such a mitzvah. This man does not observe Shabbat properly, and you must chase after him until he does, etc. In other words, the Evil Inclination's method is to lie and cheat and pretend that it seeks the welfare of a person.

I'll give you an example. Today I had dealings with the Evil Inclination. As is my custom I awakened before sunrise and I wanted to go and bathe in the mikveh. Along comes the Evil Inclination and tries to seduce me. He says: How can you go bathe in this cold weather? It's freezing outside, there's snow and ice, the water in the mikveh is frozen, and bathing under these conditions is a sin, because it may endanger your life.

I said to him: If the air is so cold, how did you get here? Did you not stay in my house all night! Surely you feel very cold. Therefore lie down in my place in my warm bed, and I will go to the mikveh.

I went to the mikveh, I shattered the ice, went down and bathed. But when I looked around, I saw the Evil Inclination next to me in the water. He starts to praise and laud me. You are a true tzaddik; there is no one as great as you!

Again he is pretending to be a friend in order to bring pride to my heart.

Who Is Chasing Whom?

It happened once that Rabbi Pinhas of Koretz went to the bet midrash and saw his students deeply engrossed in conversation. They were frightened when they saw him.

What are you discussing? he asked.

Rabbi, they replied, we are dealing with our deep concern that the Evil Inclination is chasing us.

Worry not, answered the rabbi. You have not yet reached the high level at which the Evil Inclination is chasing you. Right now you are still chasing after him.

Which Inclination?

It happened once that a certain widow poured out her sorrow in tears to Rabbi Aharon of Karlin, that the match of her daughter and her fiancé might, God forbid, might end unless she is able, very quickly, to find the money she promised to the groom as a dowry.

Rabbi Aharon asked her how much she had promised, and when she told him, he gave her the amount required.

Several weeks passed, and again the woman came to Rabbi Aharon crying. This time she complained that she could not fix the date of the wedding for her daughter since she did not have money to sew her a wedding dress.

Rabbi Aharon reflected for a while, but again gave her the required amount.

Rabbi Aharon's wife complained to him: You gave her money for the dowry to fulfill the mitzvah of "hakhnasat kallah" (helping a bride), since the relationship might, Heaven forbid, have been cancelled. But money for a dress? Does one end a relationship because of lack of a wedding gown? If you had distributed the money for the wedding gown to the poor, surely you would have fulfilled a greater mitzvah.

Rabbi Aharon replied: Yes, I reflected on that question, that it would have been better to give the money to charity for the poor. But I immediately changed my mind, and said to myself: If the request to give the money to the poor were coming from the Good Inclination, why didn't the Good Inclination encourage me to perform this mitzvah yesterday or the day before, instead of now that I want to do something good for a poor widow who is about to marry off her daughter, and to help celebrate with a poor bride so that she will not be embarrassed to stand under the huppah with an old dress?

From this thought I deduced that it was not the Good Inclination that gave me advice, but the Evil Inclination. It wanted to trick me not to fulfill the mitzvah of "hakhnasat kallah" with a full heart.

Rabbi Aharon of Karlin
1736 – 1772

Rabbi Aharon was one of the most important of the students of the Maggid, Rabbi Dov Ber of Mezritch, and the leader of the Hasidic movement in the communities of Lithuania.

His passionate enthusiasm for daily prayer was well known, and led many to repentance.

He died in the prime of life, at age 36. His writings were collected by his students.

One Must be Careful to Avoid Lashon HaRa – Including toward Oneself

It happened once that Rabbi Yisrael Meir HaKohen Kagan (author of "Hafetz Hayyim") was walking in his village of Radin in a torrential rainstorm. The street was completely empty. On the road there appeared a Jew traveling in his wagon and asked him: Where does your Rabbi live – the tzaddik, author of "Hafetz Hayyim?"

The rabbi, known for the name of his book, Hafetz Hayyim, answered: First of all, he is not a rabbi. Secondly, he is not a tzaddik.

The Jew answered in surprise: Is it possible? Everyone considers him as one who fears God and is a tzaddik!

The Hafetz Hayyim answered him again: Whatever they say means nothing, because they don't know him. I, on the other hand, know him well, and I am here to tell you that what people say about him is greatly exaggerated.

The visiting Jew became angry, and slapped the rabbi on the face.

The Hafetz Hayyim deeply regretted that he had brought a Jew to sin.

A short while later, when the Hafetz Hayyim reached his home, he found the traveler sitting and waiting for him. When he found out that he had slapped the Hafetz Hayyim on the face, he almost fainted. The Hafetz Hayyim calmed him and told him: You did not do anything wrong. I deserved the slap. I have now learned an important lesson about proper manners.

It is not only forbidden to speak wrongly – Lashon HaRa – about others – but even about oneself it is forbidden to speak Lashon HaRa.

A Special Warning about the Prohibition of Speaking Lashon HaRa

It happened once that the Hafetz Hayyim explained to his friends: I have a very special obligation to guard my tongue from evil speech. As is well known, I make my living these days from the sale of my book, "Hafetz Hayyim," whose main idea is the prohibition of speaking Lashon HaRa, in all its details.

Therefore, if I myself am not very careful regarding this terrible sin, I am deceiving the people who buy my book. And the money that I receive from the sales is in the category of theft.

The Greatest Sin – Sinning against One's People

Rabbi Yitzhak Elhanan Spector of Kovno taught: See how great is the sin that one commits against one's people!

From the Torah we learn that the Blessed Holy One forgave the generation of the wilderness for many great sins that they committed against Him.

They sinned with the golden calf. They were forgiven.

They sinned in lusting to eat meat. They were forgiven.

They sinned again in the quarrel of Korah. Again they were forgiven.

Only for the sin of the spies – when they brought a bad report on the Land of Israel, and asked to return the people to Egypt – God did not forgive the Israelite people. God decreed regarding those who left Egypt: "In this very wilderness will your carcasses fall" (Bemidbar 14:29).

From this we learn that of all the sins in the world – both sins between humans and God and sins between humans and their neighbors – repentance will remove the sin.

Only for the sin that one sins against one's people, there is never atonement. Even if one should have complete and total regret and does total repentance – there is no atonement for such a grievous sin!

Exile and Redemption

Neither He Nor the Jewish People Merited

Rabbi Zev Keetzes, a student of Rabbi Yisrael Baal Shem Tov (the Besht) from his youth, had a huge yearning to go up to Eretz Yisrael – as the Torah says, "a land which Adonai your God looks after, on which Adonai your God always keeps His eye, from year's beginning to year's end" (Deuteronomy 11:12).

Rabbi Zev made all the preparations for the voyage that one could do. He saved every single perutah that he could, he hoarded his daily food rations, sold his precious books, and in this way gathered enough money that would enable him to travel to the Holy Land. Nevertheless he could not make the trip, because his teacher, the Baal Shem Tov, did not permit it.

The Baal Shem Tov received him with an angry face, with lowered eyes, but regarding his request – permission to travel to Eretz Yisrael, he did not say a word – except to hint that he should stop talking about it.

Rabbi Zev did not understand the conduct of his teacher. Was not his love of Eretz Yisrael very great? So why did he not let him travel to the Holy Land? Apparently he did not dedicate himself sufficiently towards this great goal. Rabbi Zev therefore decided to begin right away with fasting, in order to prepare himself for this precious dream.

Many days passed during which Rabbi Zev indulged in several different and difficult kinds of self-mortification. After all that preparation he presented himself again before his teacher. The eyes of the Besht were filled with tears, and his heart was filled with pity. He placed his hand on the shaking shoulder of Rabbi Zev and said: Nu – if you are so determined to travel – may God be with you! Go up and succeed! But be very careful! Be careful that you not stumble with your tongue and with your direction!

Rabbi Zev heard the blessing of his teacher, and was filled with great joy. On Friday afternoon Rabbi Zev entered the ship which would take him to the Holy Land. The ship sailed day after day, night after night, until it reached a large settlement. It anchored and intended to remain several hours to resupply with various requirements.

Rabbi Zev looked around, and saw before him a beautiful city, draped with flowers and greenery. While he was enjoying the beautiful view, an elderly Jewish gentleman entered the ship. He had a beard as white as snow, and a leather belt around his waist. He asked the rabbi to join him in his home to make a minyan for morning prayers, to have some breakfast together, and then he could return to the ship.

Rabbi Zev agreed, and went to the home of the elderly gentleman. He prayed with great joy, because he already felt that he was getting closer to Eretz Yisrael, and the elaborate hospitality of the old man gave him great pleasure. After prayers they had some breakfast, drank some wine, and immersed in discussion.

The elderly man asked Rabbi Zev: What is the condition of Jews in the Diaspora? He related that he had heard that the terrible man Chmielnicki perpetrated horrors, and slaughtered tens of thousands of Jews. And after that a false messiah raised the hopes in the broken hearts of the remaining Jews – such that the condition of Jews in the Diaspora right now is quite bad.

Rabbi Zev replied with a joyful heart that the Almighty will not desert His people, and that the situation is not all bad. The

Jewish people trusts in Adonai, he said, among other words of comfort.

The two men were deep in discussion when Rabbi Zev remembered that the ship was ready to depart. So he ran to the ship at the very moment it began to sail.

Days and nights passed, and the ship went forward. But Rabbi Zev noticed that the ship was passing familiar places, places where they had already seen. Finally the ship anchored at the same place from which it had departed to Eretz Yisrael several weeks before. Rabbi Zev did not believe his eyes, and asked the captain for an explanation. The captain answered that while he was visiting with the elderly gentleman the ship reached Eretz Yisrael, and was now back home. It turned out that Rabbi Zev remained there two whole weeks!

Rabbi Zev got off the ship sad and dejected, went to see his teacher with shaking knees, and broke out in a bitter cry. The Besht got up from his seat, approached Rabbi Zev and said to him: Did I not say to you, and warn you, that you should not stumble with your tongue and your direction! The elderly man in whose house you were a guest was our father Abraham, the man of great lovingkindness. The hour was the time of redemption, and they waited only for you to come and bring the Messiah, and announce that the power of suffering has lessened. But you postponed the coming with your confidence that it is not the right time or place. So you did not merit to enter Eretz Yisrael. The pain of our people did not grow inside you. You did not anguish enough to understand that the Exile cannot continue even one more hour. You did not care enough about the land and the redemption of the Jewish people who are suffering among the gentiles.

Pity, pity, my friend and pupil! You did not merit, nor did the

Jewish people merit the coming of the Messiah. Let your mistake be a warning sign to the next generation. They will postpone the end of days until they feel that the strength of the suffering of the Jewish people in exile is faltering.

The Clock That Announces the Coming of the Messiah

Rabbi Dov Ber of Radoschitz said about himself, that in his lifetime he served 120 tzaddikim, and from each one he learned one moral quality. But from his teacher, the "Seer" of Lublin, the one thing he learned was to absorb the essence of vitality of the good qualities. He said: Every tzaddik served for him as an alarm clock that beat on his heart from the outside. But the Seer was a voice beating from inside his heart.

Once Rabbi Dov Ber came to a village inn to stay overnight. His sleep was disturbed by the movement of a clock in the room next door. For an entire hour his bed shook. He wanted to review orally several sentences of the Mishnah which he memorized, but the ticking of the clock disturbed his thoughts. Suddenly he had a powerful urge to dance in honor of the Blessed Almighty, in the rhythm of the clock. His soul soared, and he danced with intensity all night. In the morning the innkeeper asked him why he was dancing all night.

Rabbi Dov Ber replied: If your honor will inform me from where you acquired the clock in the next room, I will be able to tell you why I danced.

The innkeeper told him that once a Polish man stayed at his inn, and he did not have enough money for food, drink or lodging. So he left as a pledge this clock, and promised to claim it soon. But months passed, and the pledge has still not been redeemed.

Rabbi Dov Ber asked him, What is the name of the man? The innkeeper replied that he did not remember, but he knows that the man was a relative, or a grandson of some great tzaddik.

And what was the name of the tzaddik?

The man did not remember.

Again the rabbi asked: Perhaps the owner of the clock mentioned the name of the Seer of Lublin?

The innkeeper replied: I am an ignorant man, and I do not know who is the Seer. I never heard the name Seer, but the name Lublin I did hear. Now I remember. The owner of the clock told me that he was the grandson of the tzaddik of Lublin.

Rabbi Dov Ber said: You are not a simple man, or an ignorant or unlearned man. One who heard the name of the tzaddik of Lublin, and knows how to pronounce it, and anyone who knows the name of the city of Lublin, has already become connected to my holy teacher, the tzaddik of Lublin, of blessed memory. One who is connected to a holy person is holy himself.

I promised to explain to you the reason for my dancing.

When I heard the ticking of the clock in the room next door, I immediately assumed that it was the clock of my rabbi – the holy Seer, may his soul rest in peace. Every clock's sounds have an echo of the angel of death approaching. The sounds therefore arouse sadness and melancholy. But the clock of my teacher and rabbi, the Seer of Lublin, of blessed memory, announces with each click that the Messiah is on the way – which is good news.

Therefore I danced all night a dance to greet the Messiah.

Rabbi Yaakov Yitzhak Horvitz
1745 – 1815

Rabbi Yaakov Yitzhak Horvitz (The "Seer" of Lublin) was a student of the Maggid of Mezritch and Rabbi Elimelekh of Lizhensk. In his younger years he served as a rabbi in Galicia, and later settled in Lublin in central Poland.

He stood above all the other rebbes in his generation, and all the great rabbis and tzaddikim in Poland accepted his leadership without question.

His teachings were compiled by his students after his death, and published in "Divray Emet," and "V'Zot Zikaron."

Let the Messiah Come!

Late in the afternoon, just before the recitation of "Kol Nidre," Rabbi Moshe Teitelbaum spoke to God and said: Master of the Universe! Had I known that I would grow old, and the Messiah still would not have come, I could not stand the thought. But you have postponed the coming of the Messiah from day to day, even until my old age.

Therefore I ask you, Master of the Universe: Let the Messiah come now, so that you can redeem us! Not for my sake, but for your sake, Blessed One, so that Your name will be sanctified in the world.

Rabbi Moshe Teitelbaum
1759 – 1841

Rabbi Moshe Teitelbaum was born into a family of rabbis who were descendants of Rabbi Moshe Isserles (the "Rama"). He was a student of the Seer of Lublin and of the Maggid of Kozhnitz.

From 1808 until his death he served as an instructor in Ujhely, Hungary. In the communities of Galicia and Hungary he was known as a miracle worker, and myriads came to receive his blessing.

His book "Yismah Moshe" on the weekly portions of the Torah, the Prophets and Writings (three volumes) was reprinted many times. His other books include "Heishiv Moshe," "Yayn HaRekah," and "Siah S'funim."

Next Year in Jerusalem!

A certain Jew rented a tavern in a village from a Polish landowner. During the Pesah Seder, when this Jew came to the sentence, "Next year in Jerusalem!" he recalled his loneliness in a village far from his Jewish brothers and sisters, and was extremely sad. But suddenly he began to get excited and cried out in a loud voice: "Next year in Jerusalem!," "Next year in Jerusalem!"

At that very moment, the landowner was passing by and heard the screaming. He came into the tavern and asked the Jew: How come you are screaming and awakening the entire village from their sleep?

The Jew explained to him the whole story of the long Jewish exile, and the hope for the coming of the Messiah, and explained the expression, "Next year in Jerusalem!"

The landowner replied: If that is the case, Mr. Jew, then listen to me. I will give you until next Passover, a year from now, and if you do not fulfill your holiday promise to go up to Jerusalem, you will be banished in shame from this village.

A year passed – and the Messiah still had not arrived. When Pesah came, the landowner summoned the Jew and asked him:

Nu, Jew-boy, what about your promise "Next year in Jerusalem?" Didn't I warn you! Now you have a choice. Either you leave the village and go immediately to your Jerusalem, or you abandon your faith and stop announcing "Next year in Jerusalem!"

The Jew stood, sad and depressed, and turned to God: Master of the Universe, it is well known to You, that I am ready to degrade myself before this cruel Polish landlord. But what about Your great name and reputation? Why should the gentiles say that the Jews are liars, that every year they say "Next year in Jerusalem!" – and do not go there?

Send us, God, Your righteous Messiah, and it will be "Next year in Jerusalem!"

Why Do We Need Two Messiahs?

Rabbi Shmuel Mohliver, one of the leaders of the Hovevei Zion movement, and a founder of religious Zionism, was once asked by a friend: Why was it necessary to have two emissaries – Moshe and Aharon – in order to bring the Israelite nation out of Egypt? Would not one have been sufficient?

Rabbi Mohliver replied: The future redemption will also have two messiahs. At first there will be Messiah ben Yosef, and then later Messiah ben David – because two Messiahs are required: One to take the Jewish people out of the Exile. The other to take the Exile out of the Jewish people.

All Gentiles – to Eretz Yisrael

Rabbi Nahum of Chernobyl once stayed overnight at an inn. At midnight he awakened and read "Tikkun Hatzot" with bitter tears. The other guests at the inn were awakened, so the innkeeper rushed to Rabbi Nahum and asked: Why is the good rabbi crying? Are you in pain?

No, answered the rabbi. I am mourning the destruction of the ancient Temple, and the Exile of our people from Jerusalem. Long ago we lived in our own beautiful land – but we were driven out. Long ago we had a beautiful temple – but it was destroyed. I am asking God to send us the messiah to take us out of the Exile and bring us to our own land – Eretz Yisrael. Are you ready to go up and live in the Land?

I am ready, but I will ask my wife, answered the innkeeper.

He asked his wife and returned immediately with the answer: We cannot go. We have pity on our farm, our cattle, our sheep and turkeys. How can we just go and leave everything?

Rabbi Nahum replied: Are things so good for you here? The gentiles attack us, kill many of us, and steal everything!

The innkeeper went to consult with his wife again. She replied quickly: Tell the rabbi to pray to God to send all the gentiles to Eretz Yisrael – and we will stay here with our sheep and turkeys.

Rabbi Nahum of Chernobyl
1730 – 1797

Rabbi Nahum of Chernobyl was a student of the Baal Shem Tov and of the Maggid of Mezritch, and was one of the most active rabbis who spread the message of Hasidism in Eastern Europe. He became well known among Jewish communities for his inspiring sermons, which attracted great scholars as well as simple folk. He traveled a great deal to cities of Eastern Europe, and among other activities he was active in distributing tzedakah, and was devoted especially to the redemption of captives.

His books, "M'or Aynayim," and "Yismah Lev" were widely disseminated in Hasidic circles, and were reprinted often.

Faith and Trust

The Solution Precedes the Problem

It happened that Rabbi Yisrael Baal Shem Tov (the Besht) traveled with a scholar to a place of total wilderness – a place bereft of water. The scholar was thirsty, to the point of near death, and said to the Baal Shem Tov: My holy master, I am thirsty.

The rabbi did not reply.

The scholar turned to his master again, and said to him: My master, I am thirsty, and I am in serious trouble!

The rabbi answered: Do you believe that from the minute the Blessed One created the world, and saw the trouble that would one day come to you, that God would prepare for you water to drink?

The scholar replied: My master, I really believe that!

They continued and traveled a short way, and saw a peasant carrying two jugs of water on his shoulders. When he reached them, they paid him a few coins, and he gave the scholar some of his water. The scholar drank it happily.

The Besht asked the peasant: Why are you carrying water at this moment in this barren desert?

The peasant answered him: My master became crazed and sent me to a well. From this well I carried some water a distance of eight miles, but I have no idea why!

The Besht said to the scholar: See the Divine Providence of the Almighty! God created for you a crazed official and brought you water. All this the Blessed Creator foresaw in creating the world. God created a solution for every problem, in every situation, for all time, to the end of the world.

Rabbi Yisrael ben Eliezer
1700 – 1760

Rabbi Yisrael ben Eliezer, known as the "Baal Shem Tov," or "Besht," was the Founder of the Hasidic Movement.

He was born in the Ukraine to a poor family and was orphaned at a tender age. During his youth he found sustenance as a teacher of young children in "Heder" (religious school), as a "shohet" (ritual slaughterer), as a guard in the bet midrash, and as a merchant of building materials.

Prior to his marriage at age eighteen he would travel through the villages of Galicia and Ukraine, and heal the sick with herbs and amulets. After his marriage he isolated himself for a period of time in the mountain ranges, and immersed himself in the sacred books of Kabbalah, especially the holy Zohar.

The Besht continued to amaze large masses of Jews with his extraordinary powers of healing, such that he attained the moniker of "Baal Shem Tov," the Master of the Good Name. After some time there gathered around him a throng of Jews among whom were both simple folk and great scholars, in the bet midrash of Mezhibuzh.

His teachings gave courage to simple Jews, even those who had no familiarity with the siddur. The new movement he founded, Hasidism, aroused the feeling and the religious faith of his followers to a very high degree.

It was told of the Besht that he attempted to settle in Eretz Yisrael, but on the way he felt a Divine calling to return to his home. The Besht spread his Torah, his sermons and lessons, exclusively in oral form. His students gathered his teachings, his biography and the many tales of miraculous healing, and set them to writing. After his death, his ideas and beliefs filled many books which were disseminated throughout the Jewish world. Among them were "Shiv-hay HaBesht," "Keter Shem Tov," and many others.

A Verse from Torah Is Enough

It happened that the famous poet Hayyim Nahman Bialik was sitting and listening to a lecture of a biblical scholar on the subject of the splitting of the Red Sea. The scholar spoke at length, and brought many different opinions. Some of them denied the historicity of the miracle of splitting the sea, and some of them argued that perhaps, nevertheless, there is a grain of historical truth in this story.

The lecturer talked and talked and talked, repeating again and again the same ideas.

Suddenly Hayyim Nahman Bialik arose, rapped his cane on the table and shouted: I don't understand all these learned arguments. The most scientific proof that the splitting of the Red Sea is the historic fact in the biblical verse: "Stretch out your hand to the sea, and make it part."

Trust in God

It happened that a poor Jew who wanted to marry off his daughter came to visit Rabbi Menahem Mendel of Kotzk. The rabbi prepared for him a special letter addressed to the wealthy Moshe Hayyim Rotenberg, requesting that he endow the man with sufficient funds, in the manner in which he deserved.

When the poor man came to the wealthy individual, he was received with a warm welcome. But after the poor man presented the letter from the Rabbi of Kotzk, he took from his pocket a very small sum and gave it to him.

The poor fellow was shocked, since this was not what he expected, and left the home of the wealthy man in a bitter mood. However, no sooner had he left, Moshe Hayyim ran after him, carrying all the proper lavish arrangements for the wedding. He bought expensive clothing, and everything one would need for a beautiful wedding. In addition, he brought a large sum of money, piled all these things on his wagon, and went in the direction of the poor man, finally catching up with him. He then gave him everything in the wagon.

The poor man was in shock. He said to his benefactor: Since you were prepared to help me with my daughter's wedding with such munificence, why did you at first cause me such pain and disappointment?

I'll tell you why, answered Moshe Hayyim. When you held in your hand the letter from the Rabbi of Kotzk to the wealthy Moshe Hayyim, surely you forgot that there is a God in Heaven. So I wanted to remind you that one must always trust in God.

Rabbi Menahem Mendel of Kotzk
1787 – 1859

Rabbi Menahem Mendel of Kotzk was a student of The Seer of Lublin, and the greatest student of Rabbi Simhah Bunim of P'sishcha. At age 40 he began to serve as "Admor" (community rebbe) and demonstrated advanced leadership skills. His mastery and penetrating insight into the depths of Torah became widely known, and his charismatic personality drew to him large numbers of followers. Later, in his advanced years he diminished his public leadership and spent his days in solitude pouring over his holy books. His commentaries and his manifold works are widely quoted among his students.

Hearts and Clothes

When Rabbi Menahem Mendel of Vitebsk returned from a visit to teach Hasidism throughout Russia, he was asked: What did you achieve in your journey?

I found Jews in torn clothing, and with full hearts. I found Jews clothed in gloom, sadness and tears on the outside – and total personal satisfaction on the inside.

I was able to reverse their approach. I taught them that their clothing should be whole, and their hearts torn.

Rabbi Menahem Mendel of Vitebsk
1730 – 1788

Rabbi Menahem Mendel of Vitebsk was a prominent rabbinic leader in White Russia. He was the moving force behind a group of Hasidim who made aliyah to Eretz Yisrael in 1777. He established the "Old Yishuv" (Old Settlement) of Ashkenazic Jews in Eretz Yisrael.

He first lived in Tzefat (Safed), and later in Tiberias, and made it the center of the Hasidic movement in the Holy Land.

The Power of the Blowing of a Flute

In a small village not far from Mezhibuzh lived a certain Jew who was honest and upright, fearing God and doing righteous acts, a friend of Rabbi Yisrael Baal Shem Tov.

This man had an only son, who was mentally challenged. He could not even read the letters of the Hebrew alphabet. Thus he grew up with the rest of the children of the farmers of the village – with no Torah knowledge. He would milk the cattle, mind the sheep, and blow his flute like the others. His pious father was deeply pained by this son, but he could do nothing to change his son, or to educate him in Torah and mitzvot.

When the child reached age 13 he took him to Mezhibuzh for the High Holidays. On Yom Kippur they attended synagogue services. There the youngster saw Jews all dressed in white, standing and praying, moving worlds with their crying and their wailing.

A deep feeling came over him, which he had not known before – which pierced his heart and caused him to choke. He recalled that in the fields of the village, in the wilds of nature, when he would be the shepherd to his sheep, and his heart was saddened, he would blow his flute, and this brought him relief.

But now, standing in a strange world, with all the throng looking terribly sad, he had a desire to pour out his spirit. He wanted to take out his flute from his pocket and blow it, but his father did not let him blow the flute and desecrate the sanctity of the day, and embarrass him publicly.

The shaharit prayers were completed. Then musaf, minhah, and the boy was forced to restrain his yearning, and bottle up his feelings.

When the final service of the day, N'eilah, arrived, the Baal Shem Tov tried with all his power to open the gates of mercy. But he failed, and the worshippers broke out in tears. Neither could the boy restrain his stirring feelings. He took the flute from his pocket and blew it loudly, to the terrible embarrassment of his father, such that all the worshippers were deathly frightened.

The Baal Shem Tov removed his tallit from his eyes, and with a face shining from joy, told the congregation: This simple, yet sincere shriek, which emerged during N'eilah from the flute of a village boy, who cannot read a single letter, was more important to the Almighty than all the prayers of many tzaddikim and Hasidim. It was that blast that opened up for them the gates of mercy.

The Days on Which He Did Not Eat, Those are the Best

On most Friday nights Rabbi Aryeh Levin visited the home of his teacher, the famous Rabbi Issar Zalman Meltzer, the Rosh Yeshivah of "Etz Hayyim." They would exchange words of Torah, and occasionally talk of memories of the days when he studied in the yeshivah of Slutzk.

On one occasion Rabbi Issar Zalman Meltzer turned to his worthy student and asked: How did you eat during the time that you were a student of Torah at the yeshivah of Slutzk?

Rabbi Aryeh replied: On the Sabbath I would eat at the home of so-and-so.

When Rabbi Issar Zalman heard this answer, he relaxed a bit, but after a short time, he continued: And how did you eat during the week?

Rabbi Aryeh began to list the names of the families where he ate, and suddenly stopped.

Nu? Asked Rabbi Issar Zalman. You told me where you ate on four nights of the week. But where did you eat on the other days?

Rabbi Aryeh was quiet, and did not answer. His teacher pressed him to reply.

Rabbi, he said, on the other two days of the week not one family invited me to eat.

I did not eat on those days, but don't worry – those were the days I loved the most.

Late that night, when Rabbi Aryeh was already in bed, there was a knock on the door. His family was surprised to see the rebbetzin Bayla Hinda, the wife of Rabbi Issar Zalman Meltzer, standing and shaking.

Please have pity on us! From the time that my husband met with Rabbi Aryeh, I have had no rest.

What happened to my teacher, asked Rabbi Aryeh, with trepidation.

The rabbi cannot rest, she said, since he heard when you studied in his yeshivah you did not eat several days each week. Please come back to our home! Perhaps you can calm my husband.

Rabbi Aryeh rushed to help her. When he entered his teacher's home, he found him totally shaken, pacing the floor back and forth, and could not find rest for his soul.

When Rabbi Issar Zalman saw Rabbi Aryeh, he called to him in a stuttering voice: Rabbi Aryeh, for three years you studied at my yeshivah in Slutzk – and I – the Rosh Yeshivah – did not know that two days every week you did not eat. I should have known! What shall I do when I am called to the Court on High, and they will ask me: Why did I let you starve?

Forgive me, my teacher, replied Rabbi Aryeh, it is my fault. I should have informed you.

Rabbi Issar Zalman did not calm down at all, until Rabbi Aryeh firmly promised that he forgave his teacher completely!

Honoring Father and Mother

The Mitzvah of Honoring a Father – in Every Situation

A certain man came to Rabbi Moshe Sofer and complained that his son was not honoring him.

Rabbi Moshe called the son to his office, and asked him: Why don't you fulfill the mitzvah of honoring your father?

Rabbi, my father has much money, but he does not help support me. Therefore I am not obligated to honor him.

You are mistaken, answered Rabbi Moshe. The Israelites in the wilderness accepted the mitzvah of honoring our parents, even when there was no need for each other. Fathers did not need their children, and children did not need their fathers. The Blessed Holy One provided for their needs with manna, quail and water. We learn from this that one is required to honor his father – even if his father does not fill his needs.

Rabbi Moshe Sofer
1762 – 1839

Rabbi Moshe Sofer (Hatam Sofer) was the leader of Orthodox Judaism in Germany and Eastern Europe, and was one of its most notable scholars and halakhic decisors.

Born in Frankfurt on Main in Germany, he served as rabbi in several cities in Moravia and Hungary. In 1807, he was appointed rabbi of Pressburg (now known as Bratislava, in Slovakia), a very important Jewish community. He served there for 33 years, until his death. In Pressburg, he founded an important yeshivah that became the central Torah institution in all of Eastern Europe. Most of the rabbis of Austria and Hungary were trained there.

The Hatam Sofer encouraged aliyah to Eretz Yisrael. Among his students who made aliyah were the founders of the town of Petah Tikvah.

Rabbi Sofer wrote over 100 books, many of which have been published. Among them are a six-volume series of responsa, as well as his commentaries on the Torah – all of which are called "Hatam," (an acronym in Hebrew for "Torah Interpretations of Moshe") Sofer – thus his name, Hatam Sofer.

Hospitality

Indescribable Care

Not long after his marriage, Rabbi Aryeh Levin lived in a small room with a tiny kitchen outside the house. One summer evening, a young man in European-style dress knocked on his door – and fainted. Rabbi Aryeh and his wife labored intensely until they aroused him.

When the young man awakened, he handed the rabbi a letter. The letter stated that the young man is the son of one of the Rosh Yeshivahs of Lithuania – a teacher of Rabbi Aryeh. The letter further stated that the father requested that Rabbi Aryeh keep an eye on his son, whom he was sending to Eretz Yisrael with great fear, since he knew no one other than Rabbi Aryeh, his beloved student.

It seems that on the way to Eretz Yisrael, the young man contracted typhus, and when he arrived, no one would let him stay with them lest they contract the disease too. Thus for a number of days he slept on the street in Jaffa, until that morning when he found a driver with an empty wagon going to Jerusalem. The driver brought him to the doorstep of Rabbi Aryeh Levin.

When Rabbi Aryeh heard his story he promised the young man to take full care of him in his house, until he would be accepted at the typhus ward at Shaarey Zedek Hospital.

Rabbi Aryeh rushed him to the hospital and made sure that he was well taken care of. There he received medication to reduce his pain. Back at home Rabbi Aryeh washed him, fed him (from the tiny rations that he had), and had him sleep in his own bed. He moved the bed of his pious wife into the kitchenette outside the house, so as not to risk her getting sick. For his own health he was not concerned, since, as the Talmud says, those who do a mitzvah are not harmed.

Rabbi Aryeh continued to care for him until he returned to full health.

They Will Continue to House Thieves

A certain thief who was incarcerated in a jail for criminals in Jerusalem, fulfilled his punishment and was freed. Since he lived far from Jerusalem, and had no money, he came to Rabbi Aryeh Levin – who had visited him in jail – to get some funds with which to travel home. Rabbi Aryeh and his wife treated him like an honored guest, gave him some money, and invited him to dine with them.

At the end of the meal Rabbi Aryeh said to his guest: I thank you for your visit, since you allowed me to fulfill two mitzvot. Hospitality and kindness. Since the hour is late, why don't you spend the night? Rabbi Aryeh prepared his bed for him.

In the early hours of the morning, when Rabbi Aryeh awoke to go to the synagogue to recite the morning prayers, he realized that his guest had stolen his wine cup and silver candlesticks.

Rabbi Aryeh awakened his wife, told her what happened and added: I completely forgive the thief, so that I will not be the cause of his punishment. So let us promise each other, that this incident will not create a precedent, and will not prevent us from housing thieves in our home in the future.

Of Angels and Men

This is the story of an upright and honorable gentleman who was lodged in the home of the Maggid of Trisk. The host assumed that his guest was a scholar and was delighted with his visit. He fed him from his finest foods, and hosted him with abundance.

After a few days it became clear that the man was a well-known crook. The Maggid's family was greatly disturbed that their esteemed teacher was fooled by such an unsuitable person.

The rabbi said to his family: Do not be sorry about this. Remember the story of Abraham our father, to whom God wanted to grant merit with the great mitzvah of hospitality. God did not invite important men – in fact not even people who eat, drink and sleep – but rather angels! And they tricked him and pretended they ate and drank, and accepted food and drink from Abraham in vain. And why did God do such a thing? To teach us that we perform a mitzvah with a full heart and a willing soul, without asking whom we are helping.

Just as our Father Abraham Would Do

One of the friends of the tzaddik of Jerusalem, Rabbi Aryeh Levin, tells this story: It happened once that I visited the home of Rabbi Levin in the early evening, but I found his door locked. I was told that the rabbi was teaching a class in the "Daf Yomi" (daily page of Talmud). I returned an hour later and I was told that the rabbi was at a "simhat mitzvah" (a celebration for a mitzvah). I waited another two hours, and still no rabbi. I was told that the rabbi went to comfort mourners.

I returned yet again, and this time I found two gentlemen standing in the doorway, waiting for the rabbi. I knew that the rabbi lived in a tiny room at the corner of the street, so I asked the men to let me speak with him briefly, but privately.

When the rabbi came home, very late at night, walking very slowly, he began to greet his guests who were waiting for him. I asked the rabbi if he would come with me to his room, since I wanted to speak to him privately, and that the two men agreed to wait outside a bit. The rabbi then invited them into his room, and I was very surprised. After we all went into his room, he asked them to be seated on his bed, asked their forgiveness, and the rabbi and I went outside to the street.

He then said to me: We can talk here outside. Why should we make the guests wait in the street?

Humans and Their Creator

How We Fulfill ...
"And You Shall Love Adonai Your God ..."

It happened on one occasion that a heavenly voice informed the Baal Shem Tov (the Besht) that a certain shepherd worshipped the Holy Blessed One even better than himself. He had a deep yearning to see this shepherd face to face. He had his horses tied up to his wagon, and he traveled there with his students.

He approached the foothills of a mountain on which a shepherd was sounding his horn to gather his sheep. When the sheep gathered the shepherd brought them to a pond of water to have them drink, and at that moment he began to speak in a loud voice: Master of the Universe, you created the heavens and the earth, this mountain and these sheep, the one who owns these sheep, as well as me and Your people Israel. You sustain all your creatures, and fulfill all my needs. I, who am a simple, ignorant man, do not know how to worship You, and how to praise Your name. With this horn in my hand, I will make a loud sound, as with a shofar, and I shall proclaim: "Adonai is God – Adonai Hu HaElohim."

The shepherd puffed with all his strength into the horn, and suddenly he fainted.

When he awakened he began to speak: Master of the Universe, Who created heaven and earth, You provide for all creatures, You created both these sheep and me, and You have one nation, since You are one, a nation that studies Your Torah and prays to You. But I am but a simple shepherd, who does not know either Torah or prayer, since I have been an orphan since my youth, and I grew up among gentiles, and all I can do is sing to You some of the songs of shepherds.

The simple shepherd began to sing with all his might, with great enthusiasm, until he fell to the ground weak and pale.

When his strength returned he began to speak: Master of the Universe, I blew my horn, I sang songs to You, but are these important in Your eyes, Master of the World, who brings food and sustenance to all?

What else can I do to worship You, our Father in Heaven? I am able to do one more thing, and I will do it for Your glory.

When he finished speaking, he stood on his head, flew up in the air, and waved his feet this way and that. Then he stood again on his feet, and again stood on his head, feet in the air. He repeated this over and over until he fell to the ground.

When his strength returned he concluded: Master of the Universe, I sounded my horn, I sang songs to You, I stood upside down for Your glory, but is this important to You, our Father in Heaven? What else can I do to worship You?

Last night the squire, the owner of the sheep, made a feast for his servants, and gave each one a gift of a coin of silver. Me too he gave a silver coin and this coin I contribute to You as my gift, O God.

The shepherd threw the silver coin up in the air, and the Besht saw a hand reach down from Heaven and accept it.

The Besht said to his pupils: This shepherd fulfilled "And you shall love Adonai your God with all your heart, with all your might, and with all your soul."

There is Always Something That Needs Fixing

Rabbi Yisrael Salanter taught that there are times when one can learn Musar even from a simple conversation.

Once he went out, in the dead of night, and saw a dim light flickering in the window of a shoemaker. He went inside and found the shoemaker fixing a shoe by the light of a candle.

He asked the shoemaker: Why do you stay up so late, sitting and working?

Rabbi, answered the shoemaker, as long as the candle burns, I must work and repair shoes.

Immediately Rabbi Yisrael returned to the bet midrash, summoned those who were studying and told them: My brothers and friends! I just learned a great lesson from a shoemaker.

As long as the candle burns, we must work and repair…

In similar fashion, Rabbi Yisrael, the Baal Shem Tov, would teach: Even from a gentile who speaks in simple fashion, it is possible to learn something regarding the worship of God.

He then told this tale: Once a certain gentile approached his home, burdened with a band of metal on his shoulders, knocked on the window of the Besht, and asked: Yisrael, perhaps there are some vessels in your home, such as a barrel, or a bucket, which are broken, and need fixing?

No, answered the Besht. In my house everything, thank God, is in good repair.

Take a good look, said the gentile again, surely you will find something that needs fixing.

Rabbi Yisrael Baal Shem Tov turned to his students and told them: Thus have I learned Torah from the mouth of a gentile. Even one who thinks that in his house everything is fine and in good condition, he too must search.

Surely he will find something that needs fixing.

Rabbi Yisrael Salanter
1810 – 1883

Rabbi Yisrael Salanter Lipkin was one of the great rabbis in Lithuania, founder of the "Musar Movement," which influenced the world of yeshivot in Eastern Europe. In his youth he studied at the Yeshivah of Salant in Lithuania. Thus his name, Rabbi Yisrael Salanter. He demanded that his students immerse themselves in the study of "Musar," (ethics). He preached widely, and established circles of students of Musar.

In 1848, he settled in Kovna, the capital of Lithuania, and established there a yeshivah in the spirit of the Musar movement. From 1857, he began to travel to many communities in Germany, and spread the teachings of Musar, in both written and oral forms. His many students spread the teachings of Musar in all the yeshivot that they established in Eastern Europe, and following in the footsteps of their master, fostered the ethical traits that governed relationships between people.

Rabbi Yisrael Salanter wrote many articles on the subject of Jewish law and ethics, and they were collected and published in these books: "Igeret HaMusar," "Even Yisrael," "The Light of Israel," "Imray Binah," etc.

The Merit That Results From Answering a Call

A young man visited Rabbi Yisrael Meir HaKohen, author of "Hafetz Hayyim" and known by that name. The Hafetz Hayyim asked the young man if he is a kohen or an Israelite. The young man replied that he is an Israelite.

The Hafetz Hayyim continued: Do you know why it is so important to know that I am a kohen and you are an Israelite? When the Messiah arrives, may he come speedily, everyone will come to Jerusalem, and every Jew will want to enter the Court of the holy Temple and offer sacrifices and worship there. We will all hasten to the gates of the Bet HaMikdash (Temple), and when we arrive at the gate, the gatekeepers will inspect all who come. Then they will separate us into two groups. Me they will welcome to go into the inner chamber. But you will be required to remain outside. Those outside will be very jealous, since the kohanim will merit the desired goal – to participate in the holy worship. But the Israelites will not be granted permission to participate.

The Hafetz Hayyim continued: Why am I telling you all this? Because every Jew has his special moments in his life in which he hears the inner calling which informs him: "Whoever is for God, follow me!" When you hear this call on that special day, reverberating deep inside your heart, rush and don't tarry! Do not revert to the mistake of your ancestors who missed the opportunity and lost forever a wonderful thing – which they were able to capture so easily, if only they had answered the call.

Rabbi Yisrael Meir HaKohen
1838 – 1933

Rabbi Yisrael Meir HaKohen of Radin is known as the "Hafetz Hayyim," after his book by that title, which deals with matters of proper speech.

He was a noted halakhic decisor and master of Musar in recent generations. Born in Byelorussia, he studied in Vilna, and became one of the greatest scholars of his generation. He refused to accept a rabbinic position. He made a meager living from his small grocery store in the city of Radin in Lithuania, where he made his home.

His first book was the well-known, ground-breaking "Hafetz Hayyim," based on the biblical verse (Psalm 34:13-15), "Who is the person eager for life...? Guard your tongue from evil, your lips from deceitful speech..." The book was published anonymously, and was widely and rapidly disseminated.

His major project was the collection of six volumes of "Mishnah Brurah," a comprehensive and detailed commentary on the four sections of the Shulhan Arukh.

In all he wrote 21 books, among which was "Mahaneh Yisrael," dealing with ethical norms which Jewish soldiers should follow during military service in gentile armies.

His noted humility, along with his total mastery of Torah and his acts of kindness and compassion, created an admirable role model for future generations.

A kibbutz in Israel, near Gadera, sponsored by "Poalay Agudat Yisrael" carries the name "Hafetz Hayyim."

Tears of the Tallit

It happened one summer day that Rabbi Moshe Yitzhak, the Maggid of Kelem, visited the town of Dobilin, near the city of Riga. Since Dobilin bordered on the seashore, many visitors came in the summer to bathe in the sea. Many residents of Riga came to Dobilin to spend Shabbat with their families.

One Shabbat morning, Rabbi Moshe Yitzhak went to synagogue to pray. On the way he noticed that many of the people from Riga were not bringing their tallit with which to pray Shaharit worship. They were lax in their remembering to bring their tallit with them.

Rabbi Moshe Yitzhak arose on the bimah and gave a brief talk: My friends, I want to tell you a story. It happened once on a summer day that I spent Shabbat in Riga. I entered a house to visit its owner. Someone answered the door and told me and that the owner was not home.

Where is he? I asked.

He is spending Shabbat in Dobilin.

Suddenly I heard a crying sound in the room nearby. I entered the room and saw that it was empty. The only thing I noticed was a tallit hanging on the wall, and guess what? The tallit was crying.

Tallit, tallit, why are you crying? I asked.

How can I not cry? answered the tallit. The master of the house went to Dobilin and took with him his wallet filled with much money, and me he left here alone.

Do not cry, tallit, I said, trying to comfort the tallit. There will come a day when the owner will leave on a trip to a faraway place, and then he will leave all his money, and only you will accompany him on his final journey.

Rabbi Moshe Yitzhak

1828 – 1899

Rabbi Moshe Yitzhak (The Maggid of Kelem, Lithuania) was among the leading preachers in Eastern Europe in the 19th century. From his early youth he demonstrated exceptional ability as a popular speaker. In the course of many decades he would pass through many communities and give inspiring sermons. He excelled especially in penetrating the souls of the masses in small towns and villages, who received great spiritual pleasure from the maggid's concrete descriptions of the era of Messianic days and the world to come.

Concentration

Rabbi Hayyim, the rabbi of Kresna, was one of the most notable of the students of Rabbi Yisrael Baal Shem Tov. The great Hasidic leaders of his generation praised him, testifying that all his deeds were for the sake of Heaven.

It happened once that the circus came to Kresna. Rabbi Hayyim heard that among the performers in the circus was an acrobat who was able to walk on a tight rope which was connected to two high pillars planted on two sides of a river. He joined the crowd that went to see this great wonder.

His students asked him: Why would a great rabbi, a holy man of Israel, be interested in seeing someone walk on a rope?

Rabbi Hayyim replied: I looked carefully in the face of this man at the moment when he was walking on the tight rope, with a deep river flowing beneath him, and I noticed that he gave his full and total concentration to the rope. He knew that if a foreign thought entered his mind during this walk, he was bound to fall. For example, if he thought for a second of the great financial reward he would receive during this miraculous walk – woe be he!

During that moment I learned from him, that if for a second a Jew is performing a mitzvah, he must devote himself totally, and deeply concentrate his every thought on that mitzvah – and not to think of any other matter, including a reward he might receive for doing the mitzvah – otherwise he will, Heaven forbid, take a deep fall.

The Quality of True Modesty

Rabbi Hanokh Henekh HaKohen of Alexander told this story: Do you want to know the true quality of modesty? Go see what happened to Rabbi Avraham Abish, "Av Bet Din" (head of the court) of the community of Frankfurt.

Rabbi Avraham Abish was a frequent contributor to tzedakah and was a great help to the poor. He would constantly visit the wealthy, and the merchants who came to his city to trade at the great fairs. He would pound the pavements in the city and visit the homes of the wealthy in order to collect contributions for the poor, the widows and the orphans.

It happened once that he came to one of the rooms in an inn occupied by a merchant who had traveled a long distance. The merchant sat at his desk, examined his financial records, and was deep in thought. When Rabbi Avraham Abish approached him, the merchant did not recognize him and did not hear anything he was saying. He asked not to be disturbed.

Due to the righteousness and sincerity of the rabbi, he did not press the merchant, but just turned around and went on his way.

A little while later, when the merchant wanted to go outside, he could not find his cane. He was certain that the "poor" man, who had just visited him, had stolen his cane as an act of revenge for not having received any charity. And since this cane was very expensive, and precious to him, he decided to chase after the "poor" man to take back from him the stolen object.

The merchant found Rabbi Avraham and yelled at him in a loud voice: You are a thief! Give me back my cane!

The rabbi answered him gently that he did not take his cane. But the merchant did not believe him, and continued to scream at him, and in fact beat him vigorously. The rabbi understood, but nevertheless received his attacks with love and modesty, and did not say a word.

A few days later the merchant heard that Rabbi Avraham will be teaching on Shabbat in the bet midrash on the subjects of law and legend. The merchant wanted to hear the teachings of the local rabbi, and so he went to the bet midrash. When he entered he recognized the rabbi as the same man whom he had accused of stealing his cane, and who quietly absorbed his curses and his blows.

As soon as he recognized his mistake, he fainted from the pain and shame of his disgraceful actions.

When he awakened he told some members of the congregation everything that happened. They told him that the only thing he could do was to approach the rabbi after the lecture, appease him, and ask forgiveness for what happened. The merchant accepted their advice with a full heart.

When the rabbi saw the face of the merchant coming near him, he thought he was coming again with complaints about the stolen cane. The rabbi began to calm him in front of the congregation, and said: Believe me, my brother, I did not take your cane, and I have no idea who did!

This is the kind of great modesty that the rabbi displayed. Even when he was surrounded by his congregation, who came to offer him honor and glory, he lowered himself to explain to the merchant again – without having any idea that the man was coming to appease him and ask his forgiveness for being suspicious of an innocent man and offending his honor.

Rabbi Avraham Abish
1700 – 1769

Rabbi Avraham Abish of Frankfurt was one of the giants of the generation in eighteenth-century Europe, and a teacher of many through his acts of modesty. He served as rabbi in different communities, and in the last ten years of his life in Frankfurt, Germany.

His many books include "Birkat Avraham," and "Mahazay Avraham."

The Place of Modesty is in the Heart

Rabbi Yisrael Baal Shem Tov told this story: There was an important government official who achieved greatness and wealth, but had no contentment in his life. He was always sad, and every small failure brought him great pain.

His life became unbearable, so he turned to doctors who gave him medication to soothe his mind and reduce his fear and sadness. But nothing helped.

It happened that a wise elderly gentleman met him, and saw that the official was extremely depressed. The wise old man asked him what was the cause of his sadness, and the official told him.

The wise old man said to him: The source of your sadness is pride. It is your pride that makes you think that the whole world is yours, and that everything worthwhile in the world is due to you. You will not be cured of your depression, therefore, until you learn the quality of humility, and behave accordingly. If you do not expect greatness and satisfaction for yourself at all times – you will be happy and will no longer have depression.

The official decided to accept these terms. From that time on he would no longer sit in his elegant carriage when he traveled outside the city, as was his custom. Rather he would walk behind the carriage. He would constantly repeat to himself: I am humble, I am humble. The proof is that I am walking behind my carriage.

After some time the elderly wise man met him and said to him: Your honor, this is not the way to achieve the quality of modesty. This is the way: Sit in your carriage humbly, and let humility be not on your tongue and thoughts, but inscribed in your heart. This is humility in the heart – and most difficult to achieve.

There is No Excuse for Arrogance

Rabbi Raphael of Barshad taught: In the next world I will be able to find excuses for all my sins, except for arrogance. When they will ask me when I reach the Court on High: Why did you not engage in Torah study? I will answer: I do not know any Torah. I am uneducated. When they will ask me: Why did you not worship God with prayers and good deeds? I will answer: I did not have leisure, I was so busy earning a living. If they will ask me: Why did you not seclude yourself in meditation and in fasting? I will answer: I am physically unable, and would be in danger of death. And if they will ask me: Why did you not give tzedakah? I will tell them that I couldn't, since I am poor.

But if they will ask me: You are uneducated, a miser and weak, why were you so proud and arrogant? What is the source of your arrogance? To that question I will have no excuse, and will not be able to give any answer at all.

Love of the Jewish People

What Is the Meaning of "You shall love your neighbor as yourself"?

Rabbi Yosef Zundel Salant was not only a lover of peace, but also a pursuer of peace. With all his might he would attempt to bring harmony between two quarreling Jews.

It happened once that a certain Jew opened a grocery store in the Old City of Jerusalem. A few months later another Jew opened a grocery store close by. Naturally the first shopkeeper became very angry, and his annoyance grew greater and greater each day.

Rabbi Yosef Zundel became aware of the matter. He approached the first shopkeeper and bought some supplies from him, and in the course of conversation spoke to him about the mitzvah of "ahavat Yisrael" – love of the Jewish people. It is not only forbidden, according to tradition, to hate another Jew, but we are duty-bound to love one another.

The shopkeeper understood that Rabbi Yosef was hinting to him regarding his relationship with the new storekeeper.

The storekeeper said to the rabbi: Is it possible to love a Jew who encroaches on your property?

Rabbi Yosef replied in a gentle manner and in a soft voice: It is explicitly commanded in the Torah (Leviticus 19:18), "You shall love your neighbor as yourself." This implies that you should love your neighbor, even if he is your competitor, whether he is a shopkeeper, a shoemaker, a tailor, "like yourself." In this way you show your true love.

Rabbi Yosef Zundel Salant
1786 – 1865

Rabbi Yosef Zundel Salant was among the giants of his generation in Lithuania in the first half of the 19th century. He was the spiritual mentor of Rabbi Yisrael Lipkin Salanter, founder of the Musar Movement. Rabbi Yosef Zundel was a student of Rabbi Hayyim of Volozhin, and during his entire life followed steadfastly the intellectual approach of the Gaon of Vilna.

In 1838, he settled in the land of Israel and lived in sight of the walls of Jerusalem. As he did in Lithuania, he refused to accept a rabbinic position. He made his meager living from a small business of selling vinegar, run by his wife. He spent his time in Torah study in the bet midrash "Menahem Tziyon" in the Old City of Jerusalem.

What is the Meaning of the Mitzvah to Love?

Rabbi Moshe Leib of Sassov used to say: I learned the meaning of the mitzvah to love other Jews from a Russian peasant.

Once I saw two peasants, villagers, sitting in a tavern, reeling from alcohol. One asked the other: Do you love me?

Surely, answered the other.

How can you say you love me, asked the first man, since you do not know what hurts me?

Rabbi Moshe Leib of Sassov
1745 - 1807

Rabbi Moshe Leib was a student of Rabbi Elimelekh of Lizhensk. He labored diligently in spreading the Hasidic movement in the cities of Galicia. Rabbi Moshe Leib was known for his outstanding quality of fulfilling the mitzvah of "ahavat Yisrael," loving other Jews. Many folk legends spun around his personality and his good deeds.

The main ideas of his teaching were gathered in "Yalkutay Ramal," "Torat Ramal Hashalem," and "Hiddushay Ramal."

Concern for an Elderly Postman

The mailbox of Rabbi Aryeh Levin was attached to the door of his second floor apartment.

One day Rabbi Aryeh noticed Saadya, the elderly postman, climbing the stairway, huffing and puffing uncomfortably, his heavy sack of mail pressing on his back. Rabbi Aryeh said to him: Reb Saadya, it must be very cumbersome to drag the sack of mail up these stairs.

Nu, Rabbi, answered Saadya, the years inevitably bring their aches and pains. What can I do? This is my "parnasah" (income), and part of the work of a mailman is to climb up and down flights of stairs.

If so, answered Rabbi Aryeh, from now on leave all my mail on one of the shelves on the entrance wall of the house.

But, Rabbi, your letters may get lost!

Rabbi Aryeh pressed Saadya, and did not give up until the postman promised that from now on he would leave the mail near the front door, and no longer have to climb the stairway.

Rabbi Aryeh Levin
1885 – 1969

Rabbi Aryeh Levin was born in Urla, a small town near Bialystok in White Russia; he was born in his father's elderly years. His father was a forester and a scholar. When his father died, his employer said of him: "With him died honesty in the world."

Still a young boy, he left his home and sought a place of Torah learning. He studied in yeshivot in Slutzk and Slonim, and became known as a constant student and as a prodigy.

The Location of the Holy Temple in Jerusalem

An ancient legend informs us that on the spot on which the Holy Temple was to be built, there lived two brothers. The older brother lived alone; he had no family. The younger brother had a wife and three children. Both brothers eked out a meager living as farmers. The brothers shared a field which they inherited from their father, and they divided up its yield between them in equal measures.

One night after the harvest the older brother could not fall asleep, worrying about his younger brother. He thought: My younger brother has a wife and children, and he has reaped such a small amount of grain with which to feed them.

He got up at midnight, removed some of the grain from his pile, and put it in the pile of his brother. Then he went back to sleep.

At the same hour, the younger brother also could not sleep. He worried about his older brother: He is all alone, he thought, with no family, who will gladden his heart and ease his burdens in times of need and pain.

The younger brother got up before sunrise, took some of the piles of grain from his pile, and placed it in the pile of his older brother.

In the morning the two brothers found their piles, as they left them, and neither was missing any grain. They were very amazed, but repeated their actions on the next night. On the third night, when they were transferring their piles of grain, each one to the other's, they met in the middle of the field.

They finally understood the desires of the other. They hugged and kissed.

The Holy Blessed One saw the brothers' kind and thoughtful actions at that place, and decided that on some future day King Solomon would build the Holy Temple on that very site!

We Must Pay His Fee

The wife of the tzaddik Rabbi Zusya of Anipoli, who was very poor, longed for a new dress, and he had a difficult time denying her pleas. So he borrowed money and bought her some fabric for a dress. She gave the fabric to a tailor. Rabbi Zusya thought he brought joy to his wife, but after a few days he saw that her face was very sad.

He asked her about it, and she told him: She gave the fabric to the tailor, and he sewed a lovely dress. But when the tailor brought her the dress, she saw that his face was sad. After questioning him, he told her that a short while ago his daughter became engaged, and when the groom saw that his future father-in-law was sewing a beautiful dress, he was certain that he was making it for his soon-to-be-wed daughter, for the wedding.

When he found out that the dress was not for the wedding, he became very angry, and his daughter is afraid that he may even end the relationship.

The rabbi's wife told her husband that when she heard that, she immediately told the tailor – keep the dress as a gift for your daughter, the bride. I thought to myself, she said, I am not a bride, and my husband Zusya will not divorce me if I don't have a beautiful dress. I performed a mitzvah – but poor me! I am still dressed in rags, as always, and I am embarrassed to be seen in public.

Rabbi Zusya spoke to her, and told her to forget for a moment about being embarrassed. How happy you should be that you fulfilled such a mitzvah. Did you pay the tailor extra money for his efforts?

Rabbi Zusya's wife turned to him with amazement, and asked: Is it not enough that I gave the tailor the dress? Am I obliged also to pay him extra money for his work?

Of course, answered Rabbi Zusya. The tailor is very poor, and he worked a whole week especially for you, to earn his fee. If you don't pay him, you are denying him his reward.

Immediately Rabbi Zusya borrowed more money in order to pay the tailor for his work.

Rabbi Zusya of Anipoli
1729 – 1800

Rabbi Zusya was a noted student of the Maggid of Mezritch, and the brother of Rabbi Elimelekh of Lizhensk. He worked together with his accomplished brother to spread knowledge of Torah and Hasidism in Poland and Galicia.

Rabbi Zusya was well known for his extreme warmth and love for all people, and throngs among the masses called him, with love and admiration, "The Rebbe, Rabbi Zusha."

His writings were collected in the book "Menorat Zahav."

The Value of Mud

Rabbi Yisrael of Ruzhin, in the Ukraine, was invited to visit a certain city. One of the wealthy leaders of the city hosted him in his beautiful home, and all the residents came to greet the tzaddik and receive blessings from him.

His visit was in the rainy season, and people tread in mud, and brought the sludge onto the shiny floors of the wealthy host.

The host became very annoyed. Rabbi Yisrael called him, sat him down next to him, and told everyone present this story.

A certain tax collector lived in a small village, and made a bare living for himself and his family – his wife, six children and his parents.

One year the winter was harsh. There was snow and deep cold. The roads were empty. The tax collector's income dropped even lower.

When the Festival of Pesah approached, and there were none of the requirements for Pesah in the house, the tax collector decided to go into the city and try his luck. He bought some items, and finally had flour for matzah. He brought it to the baker, who made some matzah.

In the evening the tax collector began to return home, and the street was filled with puddles and there were holes filled with mud. The wagon became stuck in one of the holes. He tried to pull it out with all his strength, but the wagon did not move. He stood and cried a loud and bitter cry.

At that very moment a wealthy man passed by in his carriage. He noticed the tax collector, and the trouble in which he had found himself, and he ordered to have the horses of his carriage loosened to pull the wagon out of the pit.

The wealthy man saw how tired, hungry and thirsty the man was, so he gave him food and drink – and he even followed him to his home. And when he saw the poverty in the house, he had compassion on him and gave him several gold coins and said to him: Go and buy yourself everything you need for Pesah – in abundance. The man rejoiced with his family on the holiday.

After a while, the wealthy man died and stood before the heavenly tribunal. The angels of destruction came in great numbers, and each one began to cry out in a loud voice: We are here to testify that this man committed many sins. And the members of the tribunal shouted out in unison: He must be sent to hell!

The rich man bowed his head in shame. His whole body shook from the terrible judgment.

But one angel arose, all white, and shouted out: I am here because of one great mitzvah that this tzaddik performed. And further, this mitzvah is equal to all his sins. As it is written, "Whoever saves one life is credited for saving the whole world."

The members of the tribunal placed all the sins of the wealthy man on one side of a scale, and this mitzvah on the other side – but the side with the sins won out.

The angel flew and brought the tax collector and his entire household and put them in the scale on the side of the mitzvah. But still the side with the sins won out.

The angel then flew and brought the horses and the wagon – but that still was not enough to change the balance of the scales.

The angel then flew and brought the mud and the sludge that were in the hole – and immediately that side won!

This proves, concluded Rabbi Yisrael, looking straight into the eyes of the host, that sometimes even mud and sludge have the power to save one from a judgment of hell.

Rabbi Yisrael Friedman of Ruzhin
1796 – 1850

Rabbi Yisrael Friedman of Ruzhin was the great-grandson of the Maggid of Mezritch. Thousands of Hasidim were attracted to him in Ruzhin. After he was imprisoned for a while by the Russian government, based on false charges, he resettled in Sadigora, in the district of Bukovina – then under the control of Austria.

He was respected by great scholars as well as by simple folk. He was the founder of a dynasty of rebbes of Sadigora, Chortkov and Boyan.

Moral Qualities

Being Careful in Regard to the Honor of Every Person

Rabbi Shmuel the Hasid was very careful in matters of granting honor to every Jew – not to embarrass or humiliate any person.

During the winter months he would get up before sunrise to go to the bet midrash, and light the oven himself, so that his students, who were coming early in the morning to hear his lecture, would not, Heaven forbid, be cold.

It happened once that the logs were wet, and so they would not catch fire. Rabbi Shmuel put his head in the oven and began to blow so that the fire would ignite. At the same time a certain Jew entered the bet midrash, joked with the rabbi, and patted him on the back.

Rabbi Shmuel did not know who it was, but in order not to embarrass him he did not remove his head from the oven – even though the fire began to burn his face and singe his hair and eye lashes. He remained that way, with his head in the oven, suffering burns and pain, until he heard the sound of the steps of the man leaving the bet midrash.

When the students entered the bet midrash, they were amazed to see the face of their rabbi with burns on his face, his hair singed, and he was groaning and sighing. When they asked him what had happened, he told them the whole story. His students then asked him: Our master, must one suffer so much in order not to embarrass someone – especially one who acted frivolously?

Rabbi Shmuel replied: Did our sages not teach: "It is better for a person to put his himself in a burning furnace rather than humiliate another person?" (Talmud, Bava Metzia 59a)

Never Humiliate Anyone

One of the leaders of the rabbinate arranged a large "se'udat mitzvah" (a meal in honor of a mitzvah), and he invited the important people in the city – rabbis and lay leaders.

When they were all seated at the table the host showed them an ancient coin and said: This coin is unique. It is ancient, from the days of the kings of Judah and Israel. My grandfather, the Gaon Rabbi Shaul Wahl, acquired it from the treasures of the King of Poland for a very high price.

The coin passed around the room from hand to hand and everyone's curiosity was aroused. One elderly rabbi took the coin, examined it carefully at length. As it was passed around the room, it somehow disappeared. Everyone looked for it, but could not locate the valuable coin. The host was totally distraught over this precious treasure, and all the guests were upset over the matter.

One of the leaders of the generation arose and suggested that a meticulous search be arranged of everyone at the table. They agreed unanimously to this suggestion – except for this one elderly rabbi.

This man said to the gathered assembly: My masters! Such a search will not add honor to anyone here. Let each person search himself carefully, lest he misplaced the coin accidentally.

Since the elderly rabbi was one of the leaders of the generation, everyone agreed with his suggestion, and postponed the search

– "on condition" – namely that if after one hour the coin is not found, they would return to the first idea – a thorough search by others of each person present.

An hour passed. Two hours passed, and no coin. Having no choice they began the search, person by person, until they reached the elderly rabbi. His face was white as plaster. He did not permit the searchers to check his pockets. They checked anyway, with force, and found the coin.

In one voice those assembled cried out: Oy to the eyes that see this! A respected rabbi, well known for his righteousness in all matters, and pious in every way – should, in the eve of his years, commit such a great sin!

With deep anxiety they finished the meal. As they were reciting the Grace After Meals in a whispered tone, the housemaid came into the room, hurried and harried, and announced that while she was washing the dishes she found the coin, mixed in with the leftovers on one of the plates.

Everyone in the room rejoiced and were overwhelmed with glee that the suspected rabbi was found innocent of this terrible charge.

They turned to the pious rabbi, and said to him: You have always been faithful and honest to us. Why did you not tell us that you had in your pocket another coin like this one? If you had done so you would not have placed yourself in this terrible suspicion, and you would not have brought all of us to the point of suspecting an innocent person!

He replied: I was not concerned with my own honor. Nor was I worried about the precious coin. But our kind host announced publicly that his coin was unique – the only one of its kind in the world – and I did not want to embarrass him by saying that I have one just like it!

A Special Ketubah

Rabbi Yitzhak Epstein, who for many years was "Dayan" (a judge in the religious court), in Tel Aviv, was matched with a young orphan whose father was murdered in the massacre in Hevron in 1929. The "shadkhan" (matchmaker) was the Gaon, Rabbi Issar Zalman Meltzer.

When Rabbi Aryeh Levin was occupied with writing the Ketubah by hand, someone said to him: There are inexpensive printed Ketubot! Why are you bothering to write it by hand?

The bride is a special person, an orphan, answered Rabbi Aryeh, and Jewish law says that one must help her rejoice with a Ketubah that is written by hand – that she should not suffice with a standard printed one. The Blessed Holy One gave me a special honor to write this Ketubah by hand.

No Longer Orphan's Clothing

Rabbi Eliyahu Zlotnik, who was a Dayan and leading educator in the ultra-Orthodox community in Jerusalem tells this story: When I was a very young child, my father passed away. Since my mother, may she rest in peace, was extremely poor, I was placed in the Diskin Orphanage. There I wore the typical orphan's clothing, which was not very attractive. On Shabbat and Festivals I was invited to the homes of my relatives in the neighborhood of Batay Broida, dressed in orphan's clothing. Everyone pointed a finger at me – "This child is an orphan." I was terribly embarrassed, and very sad.

One day Rabbi Aryeh Levin, who was called "the father of orphans," approached me and invited me to go with him to the tailor. There he ordered a beautiful new suit of clothes for me. Rabbi Aryeh chose very fine linen, and insisted that the tailor measure me several times, and saw to it that the cut was just right, like a groom at his wedding.

The following Shabbat Rabbi Aryeh turned to me and said: No longer will you dress in orphan's clothing. You shall wear your new suit, just like one of the youth of the wealthy.

It was not only the new clothing that Rabbi Aryeh bought for me that I appreciated. But also the whole pleasant experience of ordering it from the tailor, the choice of beautiful fabric, the fitting and all the rest of the experience that accompanied a tender young boy getting a new suit. It was an experience I will never forget.

Double Pedigree

It happened that a young orphan reached the age of bar mitzvah. His widowed mother arranged for him a bar mitzvah celebration, and invited the well-known tzaddik, Rabbi Aryeh Levin.

Rabbi Aryeh sat together with the boy's family, recounted to them many stories of his late beloved father and grandfather, whom he knew well. He praised their Torah learning, and their noble character. The family members derived great satisfaction from the warm tributes that they heard from Rabbi Aryeh. Before he left, the rabbi blessed the boy to grow up to be an honor and a credit to his distinguished family.

Only a half hour later Rabbi Aryeh returned to their home. The family was completely taken by surprise, and asked why he had come back.

Rabbi Aryeh explained that on his way home he remembered that the mother of the boy is the daughter of one of the outstanding scholars in Jerusalem, a man who had published several important books of Torah learning. It occurred to me, he said, that the bar mitzvah boy should take great pride also in his grandfather on his mother's side. Therefore I came back to tell the young lad that in addition to the pedigree on his father's side, he should also take great pride in his family's background on his mother's side.

Helping Widows Rejoice

A certain rabbi met Rabbi Aryeh Levin on Hol HaMoed Sukkot in the neighborhood of Batay Nayteen, in Meah Shearim, Jerusalem.

What are you doing in our neighborhood? he asked Rabbi Aryeh.

I am going to visit the widow of Rabbi Reuven Bengis, (the leading rabbi of the ultra-Orthodox community in Jerusalem). Come, join me.

Why? asked the rabbi.

It is my custom during the holidays to visit the widows of rabbis.

All during the year everyone is busy with their work, and a widow does not feel her loneliness. But during the holidays, they feel it more. During that time people are more free, and a widow surely remembers the former times when her distinguished husband was alive, that the leaders of Jerusalem would visit him, the house was stirring with visitors – and there was so much joy and celebration in her home. But now she is alone, and the holidays have turned to sorrow – and she is so sad. Therefore I am conscientious in visiting these widows especially during the festivals, to give them support.

After the death of the Chief Rabbi, Rabbi Yitzhak Herzog, of blessed memory, Rabbi Aryeh would visit the home of Sarah Herzog, his widow, every Friday afternoon, to give her encouragement. He followed this custom until illness prevented him from continuing.

On the eve of the Rosh Hashanah prior to his death, Rabbi Aryeh telephoned the rebbetzin and asked her forgiveness since he could not visit her due to his illness.

The Tefillin of Rabbi Netanel Sofer

Tefillin made by Rabbi Netanel Sofer were well known, since he was a scribe, and wrote Torah scrolls, tefillin and mezuzot. Every jot and tittle in the tefillin he wrote with purity and holiness.

After some time, Rabbi Netanel passed away, and the tefillin that he had written became very scarce.

One day Rabbi Aryeh Levin visited his friend Rabbi Abraham Isaac Kook. Rabbi Kook was very sad, since that morning the strap of his tefillin, which he had acquired from Rabbi Netanel Sofer, had torn. Obviously he could not acquire another strap, since Rabbi Netanel was no longer alive.

Rabbi Aryeh then told him this amazing story.

It is the hand of God, he said. I just came from the home of the widow of Rabbi Netanel Sofer. When I saw how sad she was I wanted to give her some money, but in order not to embarrass her I asked her if perhaps she had something to sell. She replied that there were no more pairs of tefillin left from her husband. The only thing left were two straps from a tefillin shel yad. I bought these from her for a sizeable sum – since they were surely worth it! – so here is the tefillin strap of Rabbi Netanel Sofer for you!

I Prefer to Stay in Your Home

For a long period of time Rabbi Aryeh Levin and his wife hosted and parented young orphans in their home. They educated them, and even in many cases made all the arrangements for their weddings.

When young Shmuel Aharon Yudelevitz lost his beloved father, Rabbi Aryeh took him in, raised him in his home for many years, and arranged for him to become a student in the Etz Hayyim talmud torah, where Rabbi Aryeh served as "mashgiah ruhani" (spiritual adviser).

It happened that one day a wealthy man who had no children of his own approached Rabbi Aryeh, and asked him if he could raise young Shmuel Aharon in his home.

Rabbi Aryeh replied: It will be very difficult for me to part from this child who is so sweet and blessed with such talent. But to my regret I cannot feed him properly – just some bread and a few vegetables. So if you will promise me to feed him a wholesome diet – meat and fish, etc. – I will agree to transfer to you the mitzvah that I have fulfilled until now.

The wealthy patron agreed, and the boy moved to live in his home. But after a few days Shmuel Aharon returned to the home of Rabbi Aryeh and said to him in sincerity: The food which you give me is sweeter to my palate. I prefer to remain in your home. The boy returned to live with Rabbi Aryeh.

From time to time the famous rabbi of Gur, Rabbi Avraham Mordekhai Alter, author of a well-known book, Imray Emet, visited the Etz Hayyim talmud torah, in order to test the students, and see how they are progressing in their studies.

The rabbi tested young Shmuel Aharon, and was so impressed with him that he commented on his high level of progress to Rabbi Aryeh. He is destined for greatness, he told Rabbi Aryeh.

Rabbi Aryeh invited the orphan lad, whom he had raised in his home, to his study, and asked him: Would you agree to marry my daughter and be my son-in-law?

Shmuel Aharon replied: Of course! Where will I find in this world a father-in-law better than you?

Some time later Shmuel Aharon Yudelevitz became Rosh Yeshivah of Bet Yosef, and his reputation spread throughout the Jewish world as a great scholar and educator.

Prayer

You are our Father, and We are Your Children

It happened once that the Baal Shem Tov had a vision that a harsh decree was about to come about upon the Jewish people. So the rabbi and his students held many fast days, but they could not nullify the decree. They decreed a fast for everyone in the city in order to plead for the cancellation of the decree, and the men and women gathered in the synagogue. They cried, and prayed, and recited verses from the Book of Psalms. But they could not overturn Heaven's evil decree.

Suddenly the Besht called his student, Rabbi Nahman of Horodenka, who stood near him in the synagogue. He shouted out: Thank God! The decree in the heavens was cancelled.

The Besht was sitting among his students after the fast, and he related to them that the evil decree was cancelled because of the merit of one woman in the synagogue.

When this woman heard the congregation crying, she began to speak to the Master of the Universe: Almighty God, are You not our Father, and are we not Your children? I have five children, and when they start to shout and cry, my insides turn over. And You, our Father in heaven, are so busy with many, many children, and they are all crying and shrieking, wailing and moaning – do You have a heart of stone that You do not hear their pleas and their prayers? Is it not proper that You answer us? Answer us, Master of the Universe, answer us!

At that moment a heavenly voice came down which cancelled the decree.

Ordinary Work of the Kohen Gadol

Rabbi Simhah Bunim of P'shischa taught: The Torah commands that the Kohen Gadol, as he approaches the Holy of Holies on Yom Kippur, change his clothing; then he should deal with "Terumat HaDeshen," namely, removing the ashes from the last sacrifice.

Why?

It is natural that when the holiest man in Israel, on the holiest day of the year, enters the holiest place in the world, when he is involved completely with matters of the spirit and holiness, that he would surely forget ordinary, material matters – such as praying for the livelihood of his fellow Jews.

Therefore it was decreed that when he enters the Holy of Holies, he should change his clothing, put on normal clothes, and deal with matters relating to the most basic area of normal life. Thus will he remember the worries of the Jewish people and their daily needs.

Kohen and Israelite

A childhood friend of Rabbi Avraham Yitzhak HaKohen Kook told this story: When the clock struck midnight during the period of three weeks of mourning between the 17th of Tammuz and the 9th of Av, Rav Kook – who was then only 15 years old – would close the books of the Talmud, and the two of us would go sit near the large furnace. There we would take off our shoes, sit on the ground, and recite "Tikkun Hatzot," a book of prayers for the restoration of the ancient Temple. Avraham Yitzhak would begin to cry.

After midnight we would recite more psalms in a sad, choked-up voice. He would select chapters from the Book of Psalms which dealt with the troubles of the Jewish people, which would moan about the destruction of the Temple, and which prophesied future comfort for Zion and Israel.

Once I asked him, in all sincerity: Why do you cry so much in the chanting of "Tikkun Hatzot?" After all, I too love Eretz Yisrael very much, and want to live in that blessed land. And my father most certainly longs for the day when he can go there, and awaits the coming of the Messiah!

Avraham Yitzhak answered in sincerity: Neither you nor your father are kohanim. But I am a kohen!

Blessed be the Righteous Judge

The daughter of the chief rabbi of Jerusalem, Rabbi Eliyahu David Rabinowitz-Teomim, died in the prime of life. The funeral was set for a certain hour, and the members of the Hevrah Kadisha, who knew the rabbi as one who is very punctual, stood at the appointed time, asked that the procession begin. But the rabbi locked himself in his room, and asked that the procession be delayed somewhat. About twenty minutes later he came out of his room, and gave the signal to begin.

A few days later the rabbi explained the delay.

We are commanded to bless the bad just as we bless the good. But as I was coming to recite the blessing, "Barukh Dayan HaEmet" (Blessed be the Righteous Judge), I saw that I was still having a difficult time reciting this blessing. Therefore I locked myself in my room until I was able to feel again the feeling of joy that I felt when my daughter was born. Only then was I able to bless, with the same feeling, the One who judges in righteousness.

When the daughter of Rabbi Avraham Yitzhak HaKohen Kook died, he sat shivah on a stool, and was talking quietly with several people who listened intently to what he was saying.

Suddenly a cry of pain was heard from the rebbetzin, who was sitting beside him. The rabbi sighed, and said quietly, as if to himself: I told her many times, that instead of crying so much for our daughter, it is better to be grateful to the Blessed Holy One for giving her to us for 12 years, to make our hearts rejoice. Adonai gives, and Adonai takes away, blessed be the name of Adonai.

When Avraham Binyamin, the son of the tzaddik, Rabbi Aryeh Levin, died in the prime of life, a couple from Russia who had just made aliyah, came to comfort the rebbetzin, who was sitting shivah. The couple knew the boy and were very close to him.

To their great surprise they found the rebbetzin praying the afternoon service, quietly and devotedly. The Russian man said to his wife in Russian, so that the people standing around would not understand: It appears that due to the tragedy that struck her, she is mentally confused. If she can pray with such feeling, surely she does not yet feel the terrible tragedy that has befallen her.

At the conclusion of her prayers, the rebbetzin turned to the Russian comforters visiting her: I understand Russian, and I understood what you said. You should know this: For three days one cries; after that no more crying. Had I had the merit I would be teaching my young son Torah. Since I did not merit that, I recall what is written in our holy texts: In the World to Come Moshe Rabbenu teaches Torah to adults and to the elderly; and Joshua bin-Nun teaches Torah to babies who died in their youth.

Right now my baby is learning Torah with Joshua bin-Nun.

Why is there a Public Fast Day?

Rabbi Avraham Yehoshua Heschel of Apta did not appreciate those who subjected themselves to ascetic behavior and to fasting. One day he came to a village that had decreed a public fast day because of the lack of rain. But the rabbi of Apta did not heed the decree. He went into an inn, said his prayers, and sat down to the table to eat dinner. When the people of the village heard about this, they came to him shocked, and said to him: Today it is forbidden to eat! Today we have proclaimed a public fast day. We need rain!

Why do you need rain? he asked them.

In order that our fields produce crops and there will be a good yield.

But what are you doing to make this happen? asked the rabbi.

We are proclaiming a fast, and thus are showing the Master of the Universe that it is possible not to eat or drink!

Is that the way you behave? asked the rabbi.

I think you should do the opposite: Eat and drink a lot. In that way the Master of the Universe will see that your needs are great, and then God will grant you an abundance of rain.

Requests from the Lips and Out

Rabbi Yisrael Meir HaKohen of Radin (the Hafetz Hayyim), told this story: A certain poor man, whose finances were extremely meager, happened to meet one of the wealthy men in the city. He said to him: I have a large request. Please do for me a great kindness and lend me five gold pieces. By this generous act of kindness his honor will truly save my life.

Fine, answered the rich man. I don't happen to have that much money with me right now, and I am actually in a big hurry going to my destination. Come to me at five o'clock today, and I will give you the five gold pieces that you request.

Towards evening the rich man was at home at the set hour, and waited until six o'clock, but the poor man did not show up. The wealthy man assumed that something happened to him, and therefore he could not come.

The next day the poor man met him again and repeated his request. He desperately needs the money…

Again the rich man said to him: Did I not tell you yesterday to come to my house to receive what you ask for? I even waited for you at home a whole hour, but you did not come. Therefore come to my house at five today, and you will receive the money.

But the poor man did not show up again.

The same thing happened on the third day. Again the poor man met the wealthy donor on the street, and repeated his request.

This time the wealthy man became angry, and hollered at him: I see that you do not need the money at all. Because if you did need it, you would have come to me yesterday, or two days ago, at the agreed hour. I waited for you in my home and you would have received from me the money that I prepared for you.

Here is the lesson, explained the rabbi: We pray every day "Place in our hearts the ability to understand and to discern, to mark, learn and teach... enlighten our eyes in Your Torah... favor us with knowledge, understanding and discernment..." We recite these words daily in our prayers.

Undoubtedly our Blessed Maker is ready to grant us wisdom, understanding and discernment, and to put into our hearts the ability to understand His holy Torah – at all times. But one thing God requires of us – to turn to Him, to His house, namely to the bet midrash, and there set time for study of Torah.

But in our many sins, our requests in our prayers are only requests from the lips outward. They do not come from our heart. When we leave the synagogue we indulge ourselves in the whims of this world, and completely forget everything we asked for. Tomorrow we return and ask again, and again we return and we forget.

Redeeming Captives

Learning From a Thief

It happened once that Rabbi Levi Yitzhak of Berditchev went on a tour to collect tzedakah to redeem captives. He went from city to city, but did not succeed in collecting enough money.

He thought to himself: Perhaps it is my fault. I neglected Torah study and prayer, and therefore I did not succeed in my actions. Maybe it is better to sit in my house and study Torah!

In the village in which Rabbi Levi stayed, a thief was captured. Rabbi Levi Yitzhak said to him: See what you did to yourself! Remember this, and never do it again! No big deal, answered the thief, if I did not succeed today, I will tomorrow.

Rabbi Levi Yitzhak thought to himself: This man does not despair of the punishment for his sin, but I do not persist in my mitzvah. If I did not succeed today, I will tomorrow or the next day.

Mercy

Rabbi Zusha of Anipoli would travel through many towns and villages to collect funds for redeeming captives. He would pay a ransom for Jews who were imprisoned because they could not pay their high taxes which the hard-hearted Polish squires imposed on them.

During his travels Rabbi Zusha stayed at an inn in a certain village, but could not find anyone in the whole inn. He looked and searched, and only saw in one of the rooms a cage filled with birds.

He thought to himself: Zusha, Zusha, a mitzvah has presented itself to you: to free all these locked up birds. Why are you standing there and staring? Get up and do something. All you do all day is walk around to fulfill the mitzvah of redeeming captives. Are these birds not captives? Get up and break the door of the cage, and set the captive birds free. Rabbi Zusha broke the door of the cage, and the birds flew away.

The innkeeper returned and saw the broken empty cage, and Reb Zusha strolling around. He asked him – is it you who broke the door of the cage and set the birds free?

Yes, answered Zusha.

The innkeeper screamed and cursed Zusha, and called him a stupid fool.

How did you dare free my birds from the cage? They were very expensive!

Reb Zusha replied, quietly: Dear Sir, do you pray every day?

The innkeeper stared at him in amazement and said: Of course I pray every day. What's the connection?

You recite every day in your prayers about God the verse "God's mercies are upon all His creatures!"

Mercy, mercy, cried the innkeeper in great anger, but on a fool like you it is forbidden to have mercy.

The innkeeper slapped Reb Zusha on the face and threw him out of the inn. Reb Zusha went his way to continue fulfilling the mitzvah of redeeming captives.

The Scale of Merit

Judge Everyone on the Scale of Merit

The tzaddik Rabbi Aryeh Levin always tried to judge every Jew on the side of merit. He himself related how he arrived at this high level of moral behavior: It happened once when I was taking part in a funeral, and also present was Rabbi Shmuel Kook, of blessed memory, (the brother of Chief Rabbi Abraham Isaac Kook, of blessed memory). Suddenly Rabbi Shmuel Kook left the funeral procession, which was at the beginning of its path toward the grave, and he went into a flower shop nearby and bought a flower pot.

I thought to myself: Is this the way one behaves toward a close friend, who treated him so well during his lifetime? Can he not find another time to buy a flower pot?

I approached Rabbi Kook and asked him: Is it not so that you were like a brother to the deceased? Why did you leave the funeral procession to buy a flower pot?

Rabbi Kook explained to me as follows: For many years I have been taking care of a certain man who was afflicted with leprosy, and yesterday he died. For understandable reasons the physicians, who were not Jewish, decided to burn all of his clothing and other possessions, including his pair of tefillin.

I pleaded with them, with all my heart, not to burn the tefillin. So the doctors and I agreed that they would wait until twelve noon, when I would bring a ceramic flower pot, in which the tefillin would be placed in the ground – as Jewish law requires. Therefore I had to run and buy a flower pot in order to bury the tefillin.

From that time on, added Rabbi Aryeh, I accepted upon myself to judge every person on the scale of merit.

Self Reflection

Seeking One's True Self

This story was told in the name of Rabbi Hanokh Henekh: There once was a foolish person. Each morning he had difficulty finding his clothing. Sometimes he even preferred not to undress in the evening, and went to sleep in his clothing.

One night he found a solution. When he gets undressed, he'll write down where he placed all his articles of clothing. When he awoke the next morning he read from the paper: My hat is here – and he put it on his head. My trousers are lying here – and he put them on. Thus did he do with all his other clothes.

When he was finished dressing he said: Here is all my clothing, but where am I? He searched and searched, but did not find himself.

We are just like that foolish man, said the rabbi. We do not even know where our true self is!

Rabbi Hanokh Henekh HaKohen
1798 – 1870

Rabbi Hanokh Henekh of Alexander was among the leading students of Rabbi Simhah Bunim of P'shischa, and the teacher of Rabbi Yehudah Leib of Gur (S'fat Emet).

He was known for his great wisdom and insightful

opinions. Thousands of Hasidim flocked to consult with him in his later years.

His innovative interpretations were collected in the book "Hashavah L'tovah."

The Difficulty in Reaching People

Rabbi Hayyim of Zanz used to say: In my youth I planned to bring the whole world back to Torah and to God. After some time, I realized that I would not be able to reach the whole world, so I tried to reach at least the people in my city, but that too did not succeed. After a while I hoped that I would be able to at least plant some seeds of Judaism and fear of Heaven in my own family. But that too did not succeed.

I finally decided that it would be sufficient at least to search my own soul and do repentance. However, with all my many sins, even that I have not been able to achieve.

Lift Up Your Eyes to the Heavens

Rabbi Nahman of Breslov was standing at the window, looking out at the market, and saw Rabbi Hayyim, one of his friends, running to the market to do some business. Rabbi Nahman called to Rabbi Hayyim to come in and sit for a while.

When Rabbi Hayyim came in, Rabbi Nahman asked him: Have you looked up to the heavens today?

No, answered Rabbi Hayyim.

And when was the last time that you gazed at the heavens?

I don't remember, answered Rabbi Hayyim.

Rabbi Hayyim, said Rabbi Nahman, come here and look out of the window and tell me – what do you see outside?

I see, answered Rabbi Hayyim, wagon drivers, many horses, people running to and fro.

Rabbi Nahman said to him: Rabbi Hayyim, there will be a bustling market there fifty years from now, but it will be completely different. Everything you see here will not be here in this world. There will be different wagon drivers, horses and people. I myself will not be here, and neither will you.

So I ask you, Why are you rushing so much, that you do not have even a minute of leisure to gaze at the heavens?

Rabbi Hayyim of Zanz
1793 – 1876

Rabbi Hayyim of Zanz was considered a giant in knowledge of both Torah and Hasidism. He was considered the leading rabbi in all Poland and Galicia. He served for almost a half-century as the rebbe of Zanz, and inspired many in Jewish communities in Eastern Europe.

His broad Torah knowledge became renowned, and rabbis and other great scholars visited him often to learn from his Torah knowledge.

His pronouncements in Jewish law and lore were published in a series titled "The Words of Hayyim."

Whom Shall You Seek?

A young man approached the rabbi, who asked him: Why did you come here?

I am searching for God, replied the young man.

The rabbi said to him: You have come here in vain, since you don't have to come here – don't you know that "God's glory fills the entire world?"

Asked the young man, then whom shall I search for?

Answered the rabbi, search for yourself!

Settling Disputes

From Dust to Dust

Two people stood before a rabbinical court presided over by Rabbi Avraham of Constantine. Each person argued that the land between their two properties belonged to him.

The rabbi and the two men went out to the contested piece of ground. The rabbi bent over the land and put his ear to the ground and tried to listen carefully to its message.

The two men were amazed at the strange action of the rabbi. The rabbi then stood up and told them: It's very strange. To one of them he said: You say that the land belongs to you – and to the other he said: You say it belongs to you. But the land itself answered and told me that the two of you belong to the land – as the Torah says: "You are dust, and to dust you shall return" (Genesis 3:19).

The Rabbi is not a Master, but a Servant

When Rabbi Avraham Yitzhak HaKohen Kook first came to dwell in Jerusalem, many relatives and friends came to see him at all hours of the day, presenting questions and requests, since it became known that he was available to help everyone. It was decided therefore to post on his door specific hours when he would be available. The sign was posted on his front door, but after a few days the sign disappeared. It was posted a second time, and again it disappeared. It was decided to investigate the matter, and it was discovered that the rabbi himself removed the sign.

Rabbi Kook explained: A rabbi is not his own master. A rabbi is the servant of the people. And a servant must obey his masters at any hour he is needed.

A Rabbinic Court is Best

A government official once questioned the tzaddik, Rabbi Avraham Yehoshua Heschel of Apta: In our court system when someone sues another person, he submits a written claim to the court, and the judge sets the date of the trial. Meanwhile the judge has some time to examine the matter, and when the time of the trial arrives, the two sides are represented by lawyers, and there is also an opportunity to appeal. However, in your method, the Jewish way, when the contestants come to a rabbinic court, they present their case to the judge, and almost immediately the rabbi decides. Do you think that with this method there can be true justice?

The rabbi replied: I will tell you a parable. It happened once that a wolf chased a lamb, and caught it. When it was about to consume it, suddenly a lion appeared and snatched the lamb from the wolf.

The wolf argued: This is nothing but thievery! So the two of them went for a judgment before a fox.

The fox decided: Let them share it. Half to the lion and half to the wolf. And who can divide the lamb accurately?

They decided that the fox should divide it. The fox divided the lamb into two parts, but noticed that the parts were not equal. So the fox bit off a piece that looked bigger so that it would be the same size as the other. But now it appeared to the fox that this piece was too small to make it equal to the other. So he bit from the other one. And he kept on biting off one piece after another, until nothing was left for the two litigants.

So it is in your system, continued the rabbi from Apta. You judge and judge, present lawyers, and appeal, and in the end the expenses, and the compensation for the efforts of all those involved, eat up everything, and nothing is left for the litigants.

In our system, the rabbi tries to decide, or arrive at a compromise immediately, and thus the two sides are not deprived.

Rabbi Avraham Yehoshua Heschel of Apta
1755 – 1825

Rabbi Avraham Yehoshua Heschel of Apta was among the leading students of the tzaddik Rabbi Elimelekh of Lizhensk. He worked tirelessly to spread Hasidism in Eastern Galicia and in Romania. He had a remarkable passion for the spreading of the love of the Jewish people to his students.

He wrote "Ohev Yisrael," comments on the weekly Sidrah.

Protecting the Maid

Rabbi Yaakov Berlin, father of Rabbi Naftali Tzvi Yehudah Berlin (well known as the "Netziv,") was a wealthy merchant. His home was lavishly furnished, and contained antique vessels which he would bring back from his travels to the Diaspora.

One day the maid was not careful, and when she was cleaning some glass vessels, she broke an expensive set of Porcelain dishes. The mistress of the house hollered at her and insulted her.

It is forbidden to scream at her, Rabbi Yaakov said to his wife. She is just as important as you are.

Is this possible? asked the wife, angrily. She caused such great damage!

You may demand payment from her, but you may not raise your voice to her, said Rabbi Yaakov.

If you think so, she yelled, then I am going with her straight to the rabbi. She picked up her scarf and ordered the maid to accompany her.

Rabbi Yaakov got up, put on his "kapota" (long, black coat), and was ready to go with them.

You can stay here, his wife told him. I can speak for myself to the rabbi.

I am not going to argue for you, answered Rabbi Yaakov. I know that you don't need anyone to argue for you. I am going to argue for the young servant girl. She is a poor orphan, timid and anxious, and she will not know what to say or how to defend herself.

The Secret Return of Stolen Goods

It happened once that a merchant approached Rabbi Eliyahu Hayyim Maisel, the rabbi of Lodz, and complained: I came to town to purchase merchandise and stayed overnight at a local inn. A few days later I prepared to return home. I paid the innkeeper, left the inn, and went to the train station. When I arrived, I realized that I did not have my wallet or my watch. I remembered that during the final evening, before I went to sleep, I placed my wallet and watch under the pillow, and when I left the inn I had forgotten them.

I then returned immediately and reported my loss to the innkeeper, and told him that I had forgotten my wallet and watch in my room. The innkeeper asked me to go back to the room with him, and explained to me that he had not yet had a chance to clean the room.

However, when we entered the room I saw that the room had been completely made up, and my wallet and watch were not to be found. I argued with the man, but he became angry at me that I would suspect an innocent person. I quickly understood that I had encountered a dishonest man. So I came here to you to get help in retrieving my stolen goods.

Rabbi Eliyahu Hayyim was aware that the innkeeper had been before his court before, and that he had been accused of theft in another matter. He then proceeded to invite the guest to go into an adjoining room, and asked his assistant to invite the innkeeper to his office. The innkeeper thought that he was being asked to go because of the previous case against him in court, and so he made haste to the rabbi's office.

Rabbi Eliyahu Hayyim began to speak with the innkeeper

about the charge of the merchant, and the latter became angry, arguing that he was not responsible for the merchant's losing his wallet and watch. Rabbi Eliyahu Hayyim shook his head, as if he were in agreement with what he heard, and meanwhile the innkeeper took out of his pocket a box of tobacco and began to sniff it.

In the course of the conversation Rabbi Eliyahu Hayyim asked the innkeeper if he could take a sniff of the tobacco. The rabbi took the box, took a sniff, and the conversation continued.

Suddenly Rabbi Eliyahu Hayyim arose from his seat, asked the innkeeper to excuse him for a moment, and he went out of the room to speak to his assistant.

Go quickly, he told his assistant, to the house of the innkeeper and tell his wife that her husband, who is now sitting in the rabbi's courtroom, asked her to bring the wallet and watch which the merchant left in his room. As evidence that her husband was with the rabbi, take this box of tobacco and show it to her.

In a short while the assistant returned with the wallet and watch. Rabbi Eliyahu Hayyim came back to the courtroom, returned the box of tobacco to the innkeeper, and continued his conversation for a few moments. When the innkeeper left the rabbi, Rabbi Eliyahu Hayyim called the merchant, asked him to describe some identifying characteristics of the wallet and watch, and when it became obvious that they were his, he returned them to him.

Shabbat and Festivals

Fearful of the Holiness of Shabbat

It happened that late one Friday afternoon on a blazing hot summer day, the tzaddik Rabbi Aryeh Levin saw that there was a long line at the shop selling ice cream. The shop owner was obviously very busy, and was not preparing to close his shop in preparation for Shabbat.

The rabbi went into the shop and sat down quietly at one of the tables. The shopkeeper noticed him, and was surprised to see him. He walked over to the rabbi, who said to him: What shall I say to you? You are presented with a great challenge. But Shabbat is Shabbat!

The rabbi got up and left the shop. After he walked a few steps, he turned around and saw that the line was dispersed, and the shopkeeper was closing the blinds and locking up the shop.

Several days later the shopkeeper met Rabbi Aryeh and said to him: Your few words entered the depths of my heart. From what you said, I knew that you are pained by the possible violation of Shabbat. So I said to myself: I cannot bring pain to a Jew like you. I stood the test.

Rabbi Aryeh replied: God bless you! You are a better man than I! If I were in your situation, who knows if I would have stood the test?

Faith in Every Situation

Moses Montefiore was a very wealthy man, and a very observant Jew. On Friday afternoons and before holidays he would close his office before sundown – even though he knew that he would lose much money by doing so.

It happened once on a Friday night, as he was sitting with his wife, Judith, around the table, and were enjoying a festive Shabbat meal, that a messenger arrived from one of his friends who was a business associate. The friend implored Montefiore to come and meet him immediately in order to close a very lucrative business deal. Montefiore replied to the messenger that he was observing the holy Sabbath, and for all the fortune in the world he was not willing to enter into any business deal on that sacred day.

The messenger returned to his employer, but an hour later came back again to the Montefiore home and handed him a sealed letter, written by the business associate himself.

Montefiore did not want to open the letter on Shabbat, so the messenger opened it and read it to him. In the letter the businessman warned him that if he did not come immediately, he would cease all business and personal relations with him. Even this warning did not change Montefiore's mind, and he told the messenger to inform his employer of this message: The Jew Montefiore knows that he owes a great deal to the businessman for making business connections for him, and gave him a great deal of trust. But despite all this he would not desecrate his holy Sabbath – even if he will lose the friendship of one to whom he owes so much appreciation and blessing.

When Shabbat was over, on Sunday morning, a messenger came again from the businessman to the Montefiore household, and invited him to come now to the home of his business associate.

When Sir Montefiore arrived, his associate received him with affection, and told him the following: I thank you for standing on your principles and refusing to desecrate your holy Sabbath, even after my harsh warning. In truth, I had no business offer for you. This is what happened: I was debating with one of my partners on the moral qualities of Jews. He argued that Jews love money so much that the richest of them would be ready to give up the sanctities of their faith for financial reward. I refused very strongly to accept this idea, and in order to prove that I am right, I put you to the test. Thank you for proving that I was right!

Sir Moses Montefiore
1784 – 1885

Sir Moses Montefiore was one of the leaders of English Jewry. A banker and statesman, he was one of the most important philanthropists and community leaders of the Jewish people. He was born in Italy to a distinguished family that had its origins in Spain. He was a trader at the stock exchange of London, and since his marriage to Judith Cohen, whose sister was married to Nathan Mayer Rothschild, he acted as stockbroker for the Rothschilds. The two brothers-in-law became business partners, and Montefiore amassed a large fortune in banking.

In 1824 he retired from business and used his time, energy and fortune for communal and civic responsibilities. He visited Eretz Yisrael seven times, and was very active in the establishment of the Jewish settlement in the Holy Land. He initiated the founding of the first settlement outside the walls of the Old City of Jerusalem – "Mish'kenot Sha-ananim." After his first visit to Eretz Yisrael in 1827 he became a strictly observant Jew. Montefiore worked for equal rights for English Jewry. Because of his labors for world Jewry he was referred to as "Minister Montefiore."

A Gift from God, Not a Gift from Flesh and Blood

It happened once that Rabbi Yisrael Baal Shem Tov was sitting with his students at Shabbat dinner, when he suddenly burst out laughing. Immediately after, he started laughing again. And a third time. The whole matter was amazing to his students, who had never seen him laugh like that.

When Shabbat ended, they asked him why he was laughing, and he answered: Saddle my horses and follow me, and you will understand why I was laughing.

They traveled all morning, until they reached a big city. The leaders of the city were delighted to see him, and all the people in the city came out to greet him.

After morning prayers the Besht asked the community leaders to bring to him Shabtai the bookbinder and his wife. When they came, the Besht turned to them and said: Tell us what you were doing last Shabbat evening. Tell us the truth – don't be afraid!

Shabtai told this story: I will not hide from you what I was doing, and if I sinned, I will ask that you forgive me. I make my living by binding books. As long as I had the strength I made a very good living. Every Thursday I would buy my Shabbat supplies, and on Friday in the afternoon I would finish my work. After that I went to the synagogue, and stayed there until the end of the Shabbat prayers. This has been my custom all my life.

However, now, in my advanced years, I don't have the strength to work as before. Therefore it is not possible for me to prepare all the needs of the holy Sabbath on Thursday, as I used to. So I no longer go to the synagogue on Friday nights.

Last Friday I did not have even a penny to buy my Sabbath needs. My whole life I never needed to ask for charity, and even now I do not want to take anything from the charity box, or knock on doors and beg. I decided that it would be best to fast on Shabbat, rather than be dependent on other people. I was afraid that my wife would not hesitate to ask our neighbors for candles, or hallah and fish or meat. So I made her swear to me not to accept any gifts from anyone, even if they pleaded with her. Only then did I feel good about going to the synagogue. I told her that I would remain there a bit late, waiting until all the worshippers left, so that no one would ask me why there is no candle burning in my house.

When the prayers were concluded, and after all the worshippers left, I too left the synagogue. From a distance I saw candles burning in my house, and I thought that despite her promise, my wife did not restrain herself, but accepted a gift from someone. When I entered the house I saw the table covered with hallah, fish, and wine for Kiddush. Again I thought to myself, if I get angry I will ruin the joy of Shabbat. So I held back. I said "Shalom Aleichem," recited the Kiddush over the wine, and tasted some of the fish.

Afterwards I said in a soft voice: It seems that you were not able to accept bad things from God. But she answered me joyfully that while she was cleaning the house for Shabbat, she found some old buttons made of silver and gold. She sold them, and with the money she bought all our Shabbat needs.

When I heard this, tears of joy flowed from my eyes. I gave thanks to God for helping us greet Shabbat in a proper way, and I could not resist: I took my wife by the hand, went outside with her, and we danced a whole hour in great joy. I did it again after sipping some soup, and again after eating dessert. Three times I danced with my wife that night, out of joy for God's help.

Rabbi Yisrael Baal Shem Tov turned to his students and said to them: You know, the whole heavenly family rejoiced, laughed and danced with them. And I laughed in joy too!

The World To Come – for an Etrog

The Gaon Rabbi Eliyahu of Vilna was prepared, for the sake of "Hiddur Mitzvah" (doing a mitzvah in a beautiful way), to sell not only the shirt off his back, but also his place in the world to come.

It happened once, in a year of drought, that there was no etrog to be found. The entire city was in an uproar. A congregation without an etrog? The city leaders gathered for a special meeting and decided: For the city not to have an etrog, that's bad enough. But it cannot be that the Gaon will be without an etrog!

So they sent a special messenger, and demanded that he find and bring back an etrog for the Gaon – even at an exorbitant price. The messenger traveled from city to city. He turned over every stone until he was exhausted – but did not find one. However, on his way back he came across an inn, and found that the innkeeper had a very beautiful etrog. He asked to buy the etrog, but the innkeeper refused, even for a huge sum of money. Finally the messenger revealed to the innkeeper that the etrog was for the Gaon of Vilna. The innkeeper listened and said: For the Gaon of Vilna I am ready to give my etrog – for free. The only condition is that I receive in return for the observance of the mitzvah of etrog, the Gaon's place in the World to Come.

Having no choice the messenger agreed to the condition and returned to Vilna, although very sad. The Gaon must be told about the condition before he makes the blessing over the etrog. And how can he explain to him that he made a trade for his place in the World to Come?

When the Gaon heard about the trade, his face shone brightly with joy, and he said: It would have been worth giving my entire portion in the World to Come, as long as I can fulfill the mitzvah of etrog in all its details.

Blessing a Horse

Rabbi Mordekhai of Naskiz was very poor. All year he scrimped and saved so that he could have enough money to buy a beautiful etrog for the Festival of Sukkot.

It happened once that he traveled to the city to buy an etrog for ten shekalim, and noticed a Jew standing and crying. He asked why, and the man answered: I am a water-carrier in a nearby town. I had a wagon and a horse, and some barrels to bring water from the well in the field. From selling these I was just about able to provide for my family. But a terrible thing happened. On the way to the city my horse fell over and died. Now I cannot move from this spot. What troubles I have! How can I provide for my family?

Rabbi Mordekhai gave the water-carrier his pouch of money, returned to his home with no money and no etrog. But his face was cheerful. He turned to God and said: Almighty God, I thank You for helping me find an etrog so beautiful that it has no equal! This year the Jewish people will observe the Festival of Sukkot – with an etrog. Some will have a fine etrog – and others will an exceptionally beautiful etrog. And I will celebrate the holiday with a horse. And I will make a blessing over the horse.

Rabbi Mordekhai of Naskiz
1848 – 1900

Rabbi Mordekhai of Naskiz devoted himself to the spread of Hasidism throughout the Jewish world. He became famous as a miracle worker, and attracted many of the simple folk. He served as a teacher in several communities, and from 1889 until his death he lived in Naskiz (northeast of Lublin).

His essays on the Torah were collected in the book "Rishpay Aish."

The Etrog that Became Unfit

One year there was a dearth of etrogs, and with great difficulty the rabbi obtained just one etrog for the entire community of Berditchev. Naturally the etrog was kept in the home of the tzaddik Rabbi Levi Yitzhak, and everyone in the city had to go to his home and make the blessing over the etrog.

The tzaddik had a longtime servant. The servant thought to himself: Right after the rabbi makes the blessing, next all the Hasidim and the important people, and after them the wealthy and the officers. By that time, when it's my turn, it will be evening, and what can I do? Am I not a Jew like them?

The servant decided that while the tzaddik was bathing in the mikveh, reciting all the special prayers, he would secretly take the etrog and make the blessing over it before all the others.

And so it was. When the sun rose on the morning of the first day of the Festival of Sukkot, and the tzaddik went to bathe in the mikveh, the servant secretly took the etrog to make the blessing over it. But – bad luck. Out of fear that someone would notice him, his hands shook, and the etrog fell on the ground. The "pittum" (stem) broke off, and the etrog became unfit. No one could use it to make the blessing over it!

The servant almost fainted from sorrow and regret, and he did not know what to do. Not only would his shameful act become known – that he wanted to bless over the etrog before the tzaddik – but also that he dropped the etrog and it broke, making it unfit for Rabbi Levi Yitzhak to bless over it.

When the tzaddik came to take the etrog in his hand and make the blessing over it, the servant told him, in heavy tears, what had happened. Naturally he expected the rabbi to be very angry. But the rabbi did not get angry at all. He took the etrog in his two hands, and with great enthusiasm, as he always did in matters of holiness, said to the Blessed Holy One: Master of the Universe, see how precious our commandments are to Your people Israel. A simple Jew like my servant rushed to bless the etrog before me – so that he could be counted among all those who run to be the first to perform a mitzvah.

The Extra Holiness of the Shamash Candle

From the beginning of the month of Kislev, the local sainted rabbi would bring the young students, including his own, into his home and tell them stories about the miracle of Hanukkah. He would sit among the youngsters, and together with them would construct a Hanukkah menorah with small saws and pen knives, glue and wooden slats. Hasidim and other community leaders would claim that the shape of the Hanukkiah of the holy rabbi was just like the shape of the menorah of the holy Temple. Not the menorah that fell into the hands of the Romans during the destruction of the temple, but rather the one that went up to heaven – and when the Redeemer comes, will light up the path for those redeemed.

The menorah was finished in time for the first light of Hanukkah. Hasidim came from near and far, and the enthusiasm was enormous. Prior to the lighting of the candle, the tzaddik would teach some words of Torah.

The Torah says "When you light the candles" (Numbers 8:2), the Torah uses the Hebrew word "B'ha-alotekha," meaning "lift up." Why lift up? Because when one lifts up the candles, one must also lift up oneself, meaning, in dedication.

He continued, with enthusiasm: Are all of us ready with the commitment of Mattathias and his sons, as in the story of Hanukkah? The group of Hasidim and their children who helped build the Hanukkiah answered: We are ready! Then they would break out in song and dance.

When the moment of lighting arrived, the tzaddik spoke about the menorah of Hanukkah that they built for that year. He counted the different pieces and opened the base on which the eight holders were prepared, and in them eight cups filled with pure oil, with wicks dripping in oil.

The tzaddik said: The strength of the holders is that they all rest on one base which unites them and brings them to a high level of holiness. And that each wick burns in its own cup, supported on the base which makes them all rise on one stick. Therefore we blessed the candles as if they were one – "to kindle the light of Hanukkah" – namely that all eight lights are as one candle, all of which are holy.

In the hushed silence which reigned, there was heard the voice of the grandson of the elderly Pinhas. The child called out aloud: How about the shamash candle? What is its purpose?

The tzaddik replied: The holiness of the shamash candle is none less than the holiness of the other candles, and, in fact, even greater. Because one is permitted to use the light of the shamash – while one is only allowed to look upon the light of the other candles. This is the merit of the woodchoppers and the drawers of water – who, thanks to them the kohanim were able to offer the sacrifices on the holy altar.

As he turned to his grandson, the tzaddik added this: Our highest hope is that you will be among the "shamashim" who bring the redemption.

No Need for Police

On one Pesah eve Rabbi Levi Yitzhak of Berditchev took a walk with his servant in the streets of the city. He met a peasant, one of the tax smugglers, and asked him: Do you have contraband that was brought from across the border?

Of course! All you want.

Rabbi Levi Yitzhak continued on his way, and met a Jew whom he asked: Do you have hametz in your house?

Now? answered the Jew in shock. It is the eve of Pesah! Rabbi Levi Yitzhak continued on his way and asked another Jew the same question. He answered: Rabbi, are you crazy? It's almost Pesah!

Rabbi Levi Yitzhak raised his eyes to Heaven and proclaimed: Master of the Universe! How much do Your people Israel cling to your commandments and how careful they are to obey them! The Czar of Russia, the mighty King, posts police and tax collectors without number in every corner of the country, and on the borders of his huge kingdom. They guard that no one smuggles merchandise without paying tax. Nevertheless much merchandise is smuggled into the country with no difficulty, and no taxes.

And you, Master of the Universe, wrote in Your Torah, "No hametz may be found … in all your territory" (Exodus 13:7), and yet you place no police or soldiers to guard us – and on the eve of Pesah no hametz is found in any Jewish home!

Shekhinah

Clinging to the Shekhinah

Rabbi Avraham Yitzhak HaKohen Kook was honored with the planting of the first sapling during the founding celebration of Moshavah Magdiel.

The rabbi threw down the shovel that they handed him, and began to dig the earth with his own hands, with great excitement and trembling.

The residents were surprised at the rabbi's action, which he explained thus: When I took hold of this tender plant in my hand, I recalled the words of the midrash (Vayikra Rabbah 25), "After Adonai your God shall you walk ... and cling to Him" (Devarim 13:5). Is it possible for a human being to rise to heaven and cling to the Shekhinah, about Whom it is written, (Devarim 4:24): "Adonai your God is a consuming fire"? From the beginning of the creation of the world the Blessed Holy One was involved only in planting, as it is written, "The Lord God planted a garden in Eden" (Genesis 2:8).

You, also, when you enter the Land, you shall first and foremost, plant – "When you come into the Land, you shall plant any tree for food ..." (Leviticus 19:23).

When I began to dig in the ground, I remembered these words of our sages, of blessed memory, and I felt as if I were clinging to the Shekhinah, and a great trembling came upon me.

The Shekhinah in Exile

After he returned home from prayer at the end of Yom Kippur, Rabbi Simhah Bunim of P'shischa told his followers: It happened once that a prince rebelled against his father, and was sent into exile. After a while the king took pity on his son, and ordered that he be found. One of the messengers found the prince in a village tavern, dancing barefoot in a torn cloak among drunken farmers. He bowed before the prince and said: I was sent by your father to ask your wishes. Whatever they may be, he is prepared to fulfill them.

The prince broke out in tears and said: If only I had some warm clothing and a pair of strong boots – I would be happy.

See, said the rabbi, we whine over the trifles of the hour – and forget that the Shekhinah is in exile.

Rabbi Simhah Bunim of P'shischa
1767 – 1827

Rabbi Simhah Bunim of P'shischa was one of the most important students of the Seer of Lublin. Later he was close to "the holy Jew" of P'shischa. When the latter died in 1813, Rabbi Simhah Bunim took his place and continued the work of his master in Hasidism. Among the thousands of his students were many giants in Torah and well-known rebbes. The best known of them was Rabbi Menahem Mendel of Kotzk and Rabbi Yitzhak Meir Alter of Ger.

Even the Shekhinah Cries

Rabbi Dov Ber of Mezritch was taking a walk with his friends. He saw a little girl hiding behind a wide tree stump, crying bitterly. He said to her: Little girl, why are you crying?

She replied: We were playing hide-and-seek. It was my turn to hide, so I hid. But my friends are not coming to search for me and find me.

When the rabbi heard the little girl's answer, tears dropped down his cheeks, and he cried with her. His friends were surprised: Why is our rabbi crying because little children are playing a game? And what is so special about the little girl's answer?

The rabbi answered them: From the answer of the little girl I learned a lesson – that I can hear the sound of crying of the Shekhinah. As it were, the Shekhinah is crying and saying: I hid my face, but no one is searching for me. In vain am I hiding, and waiting for someone to come and search for me. For this am I crying.

Rabbi Dov Ber
1704 – 1772

Rabbi Dov Ber, "The Maggid of Mezritch," was a Hasidic leader from 1760 to 1772, and the one who inherited Hasidic leadership from Rabbi Yisrael Baal Shem Tov. He became known initially as a "maggid," namely, as an itinerant preacher in different cities in Galicia (in southeast Poland). Later he settled in Mezritch, in the

Ukraine. During his active period, Mezritch became the main center of the Hasidic movement.

The collection of his sermons on the Tanakh, and his essays on the Talmud and the Zohar were published as "Maggid D'varav L'Yaakov," and in a later edition as "Or Torah."

No Intention to Show Tricks

The family of Rabbi Eliyahu, the Gaon of Vilna, was deeply worried that his intense commitment to his studies would become harmful to his health. So they asked of the Maggid of Dubnov, whom the Gaon revered and for whom he had great affection, to come and try, in his wisdom, to influence him, that he let himself rest more from time to time.

Rabbi Eliyahu was happy to visit the Maggid of Dubnov, who advised him thus: Rabbi Eliyahu, said the Maggid, it is no trick for a person not to leave his home, and sit closeted in his room and occupy himself with Torah day and night – and become a Gaon. However, if he pauses periodically from his study, and goes for a walk in the marketplace, and sees how beautiful the world is, and does some trading with different merchants, – and then returns to his study and becomes a Gaon – that is a real trick!

The Gaon answered the Maggid in brief: I did not enter this world to show tricks.

Rabbi Eliyahu Kramer
1720 - 1797

Rabbi Eliyahu Kramer, the Gaon of Vilna, was born in Vilna, the capital of Lithuania, where he lived and worked until his death. He was among the greatest

Torah scholars of later generations. His capacity for learning was enormous in all aspects of Torah. He was also a scholar in secular knowledge, and did not hesitate to use it to help him understand Torah matters. When he was 60 years old, he tried to make aliyah to Eretz Yisrael, but his effort failed. Nevertheless he encouraged many of his pupils to make aliyah, and after his death, some of his best students settled in Tzefat and Jerusalem.

Known as the GRA (Gaon Rabbi Eliyahu), he was famous for his modesty and his humble lifestyle. He distanced himself from the vanities of this world, and was rigorous in piety. He wrote more than 70 books in different fields: commentaries on the Bible, on the Mishnah, the Babylonian and Jerusalem Talmuds, interpretations of the Shulhan Arukh, explanations of the Zohar, rules of Hebrew grammar, studies on the geography of Eretz Yisrael, on mathematics, astronomy, and more.

The Days on Which He Did Not Eat, Those are the Best

On most Friday nights Rabbi Aryeh Levin visited the home of his teacher, the famous Rabbi Issar Zalman Meltzer, the Rosh Yeshivah of "Etz Hayyim." They would exchange words of Torah, and occasionally talk of memories of the when he studied in the yeshivah of Slutzk.

On one occasion Rabbi Issar Zalman Meltzer turned to his

worthy student and asked: How did you eat during the time that you were a student of Torah at the yeshivah of Slutzk?

Rabbi Aryeh replied: On the Sabbath I would eat at the home of so-and-so.

When Rabbi Issar Zalman heard this answer, he relaxed a bit, but after a short time, he continued: And how did you eat during the week?

Rabbi Aryeh began to list the names of the families where he ate, and suddenly stopped.

Nu? asked Rabbi Issar Zalman. You told me where you ate on four nights of the week. But where did you eat on the other days?

Rabbi Aryeh was quiet, and did not answer. His teacher pressed him to reply.

Rabbi, he said, on the other two days of the week not one family invited me to eat.

I did not eat on those days, but don't worry – those were the days I loved the most.

Late that night, when Rabbi Aryeh was already in bed, there was a knock on the door. His family was surprised to see the rebbetzin Bayla Hinda, the wife of Rabbi Issar Zalman Meltzer, standing and shaking.

Please have pity on us! From the time that my husband met with Rabbi Aryeh, I have had no rest.

What happened to my teacher, asked Rabbi Aryeh, with trepidation.

The rabbi cannot rest, she said, since he heard when you studied in his yeshivah you did not eat several days each week. Please come back to our home! Perhaps you can calm my husband.

Rabbi Aryeh rushed to help her. When he entered his teacher's home, he found him totally shaken, pacing the floor back and forth, and unable to find rest for his soul. When Rabbi Issar Zalman saw Rabbi Aryeh, he called to him in a choppy voice: Rabbi Aryeh, for three years you studied at my yeshivah in Slutzk – and I – the Rosh Yeshivah – did not know that two days every week you did not eat. I should have known! What shall I do when I am called to the Court on High, and they will ask me: Why did you let your student starve?

Forgive me, my teacher, replied Rabbi Aryeh, it is my fault. I should have informed you.

Rabbi Issar Zalman did not calm down at all, until Rabbi Aryeh firmly promised that he forgave his teacher completely!

Teshuvah

Trying Very Hard to Return in Full Repentance

On the eve of Yom Kippur, after the final afternoon meal, Rabbi Naftali of Ropshitz went into his room. The time came for the recitation of Kol Nidre, yet he would not come out of his room. Many Hasidim approached his son, Rabbi Eliezer, to find out what is wrong. His son enter the room, and found him crying bitterly.

Abba, asked his son, Why are you crying here in your room, and not going to the bet midrash for Kol Nidre?

I am embarrassed to enter the bet midrash, answered his father, with intense weeping. The many Hasidim who are waiting for me, answered Rabbi Naftali, think that I am holy and pure. But I know the truth about myself, and about my deeds. Every day I promise to return in full repentance, and that I will change my actions for good. A year passed, and I have not returned in repentance. So I promised the Blessed Holy One that during the Ten Days of Awe I would examine my deeds and no longer sin. And now I stand, the eve of Yom Kippur, and I know that still I have not returned in repentance.

And again Rabbi Naftali broke out in tears.

Rabbi Eliezer, his son, said to him: Abba, come with me to the bet midrash, and I am certain that now you will return in full repentance.

After much pleading and promising by his son, finally Rabbi Naftali entered the bet midrash and began to recite Kol Nidre.

Rabbi Naftali Tzvi of Ropshitz
1760 - 1827

Rabbi Naftali Tzvi of Ropshitz was a leading student of Rabbi Elimelekh of Lizhensk (The Seer of Lublin), the Maggid of Kuzhnitz, and Rabbi Mendel of Rimanov. He became famous as having a penetrating mind, and an incisive expression of thought. Thousands of Hasidim became his followers, and his thoughtful essays were well known.

His writings include "Zera Kodesh," and "Ayalah Sh'luhah."

Question in a Dream

It happened that in a certain city there was a person who constantly slandered others, and continued to annoy all the people in the city with his slander of the mayor of the city. The slanderer was despised by all the residents, and was fearful of walking alone in the city, even during daylight. Therefore he hired two gentile guards, who accompanied him at all times, at the instruction of the mayor of the city.

Once the slanderer went to the mayor, who lived very far from the city, together with his two guards. On the way they stopped at an inn. The man recited the afternoon prayers, and while he was saying the "Shemoneh Esray," he came to the section that said: "Forgive us, our Father, for we have sinned" and suddenly he realized that he is a sinner because of all his slandering. He became exceedingly sad. He stopped his prayer and decided to turn away from his evil deeds – namely, he would immediately return home and not go to the mayor in order to slander him. He gave a great deal of thought to these matters.

The two guards who were accompanying him saw that he was pausing for a long time during the "Shemoneh Esray" and that he was sighing quietly. They were confused and asked him: What happened that you paused during the prayers and started to cry?

The man answered them, saying that he did not feel well, and wanted to go back home. But the guards did not believe him, and continued walking.

When they arrived at the home of the mayor of the city, the man kept his promise, and would not pass along any negative reports. The mayor became angry, and beat him vigorously, and in the end threw him out.

On his way home the man heard the sound of loud wailing. He approached the place where the sound was coming from – and it turns out that a naked woman was standing there, screaming in a bitter voice, and told him: I am from such-and-such a village, and tonight is the end of my menstrual period. I came with my husband to bathe in the river, as Jewish law demands at the end of the menstrual period, and my clothes were in the wagon. Suddenly the horse began to run away with the wagon, and with it, all my clothing. My husband ran after it, and I am here alone, naked, and I am freezing.

The man quickly took off his overcoat and covered the woman. Then he took her to her home. After that he went to her husband and told him that he saved his wife, and that she is already home.

The next day the man became sick and stayed in bed. That night he died.

Many people participated in the funeral, since they were so happy that he died, and that they were relieved of this terrible slanderer.

Several days after his death, the husband of the woman whom the slanderer had saved, came to ask the rabbi if it were permissible to live with his wife – since she was naked in the presence of the slanderer. She swore that he did not molest her.

The rabbi did not know how to reply, and so asked him to come back the next day. That night the rabbi asked a question in his dreams, to be answered by God, what is the ruling regarding this woman.

In his dream the entire story was told to him: How the man repented of his slandering in full repentance, and then stood the test with the mayor of the city, and did not slander anyone – despite the beating that he received. Therefore God provided him the opportunity to perform the mitzvah of "pikuah nefesh" (saving a life) – which is the greatest of all the mitzvot – and that he fulfilled the mitzvah in all its details, and did not let his evil inclination lead him astray.

Thus he died, innocent and a complete Baal Teshuvah, and an honored place was ready for him in Gan Eden (Heaven).

Truth and Falsehood

Love of Truth

R abbi Eliyahu Hayyim Maisel, the rabbi of Lodz, was
known as one who loved every human being, but more
than anything he loved truth. When someone complained that
Ploni or Almoni deceived him, he would study the matter in
great detail to clarify the matter and find out the full truth. In
such matters he never distinguished between Jews and gentiles.

It happened once that a certain gentile came to him and began
to pour out his heart.

I am a resident of Lodz, he said, and I live in a Polish
neighborhood. In the rebellion of Poland against Czarist Russia
I was among those who rebelled, and in fact I served as their
treasurer. At the end of the rebellion I had in my possession some
ten thousand rubles. It was impossible for me to deposit them in
any bank, lest it become known to the authorities. So I hid the
money in the basement of my home. I guarded the money with
extreme care, and from time to time I would go to the basement
at midnight and count the money. Several years passed, the
money remained hidden in my basement, and no one knew a
thing about it.

However, a few days ago I went at night to the basement, and
discovered that the money has disappeared.

Rabbi Eliyahu inquired, with great sympathy: Do you suspect
someone who might have stolen the money?

Forgive me, Rabbi, answered the gentile, if I say to you in all candor, that I suspect a certain Jew. One of my neighbors is Jewish, a poor carpenter, who all his life lived in poverty. His wife and children wore old, torn clothing – and suddenly he began to live a lavish lifestyle. He acquired new furniture and beautiful clothing, for himself and all the members of his family, and I…

Rabbi Eliyahu interrupted him: Did you ask this person how suddenly he became a wealthy man?

Yes, answered the man. Not only did I ask, but all the neighbors were amazed at the change. He answered that one of his bachelor uncles died and left him a large inheritance. But both I and the neighbors are very doubtful of the truth of this story. I plead with you, with all my heart, to help find out who is the thief.

Rabbi Eliyahu Hayyim promised the man that would look into the matter. As soon as the man left his house, Rabbi Eliyahu called the carpenter to speak with him. The carpenter hurried to come, and Rabbi Eliyahu received him graciously and began a discussion.

I have heard that you were fortunate enough to become a wealthy man. Why then did you not come to me, as all the other wealthy people, to contribute to our charity fund that I administer?

The face of the carpenter paled, and he became defensive.

You are absolutely right, Rabbi. I did not act justly or appropriately, but surely it is not too late.

I heard, continued Rabbi Eliyahu, interrupting the man, that one of your relatives left you a large inheritance. Was your relative very wealthy?

Yes, answered the carpenter, extremely so.

Did he not leave some of his fortune to others? asked the Rabbi.

The carpenter began to stutter, and Rabbi Eliyahu Hayyim understood that the matter of the inheritance was a big lie. He then turned to the carpenter and whispered to him.

You should know that I have called you here today for your own good – in order to save you from a dangerous situation that may happen to you. People in town are saying that you are spending money in town with counterfeit money. And of course you know what harsh punishments await those who commit such a crime!

The carpenter's face turned green with fright. He shook with fear, and turned to the Rabbi and began to explain.

Run home immediately, the rabbi told him, and bring all the money to me.

The carpenter obeyed the rabbi, and immediately handed to him all the money that was in his home.

From now on, warned Rabbi Eliyahu Hayyim, do not touch the money of others! The money is not counterfeit, and it does not belong to you.

The next day Rabbi Eliyahu returned the money to the gentile.

Rabbi Eliyahu Hayyim Maisel
1821 – 1912

Rabbi Eliyahu Hayyim Maisel was among the leaders of his generation in Europe in the second half of the 19th century, and in the beginning of the 20th century. He was a many-faceted leader of Jewish Poland during many decades. Even in his youth he was recognized as an exceptional scholar. At age 13 he was ordained as a rabbi. By the time he was 20, he became the rabbi of

Horodok, the city of his birth (near Vilna). After two years he left the active rabbinate, and devoted the next 20 years to intensive study of Torah.

In 1873 he was appointed to the position of rabbi of the large Jewish population of Lodz, in northwest Poland. He remained in that position until his death. Besides his reputation as a great scholar in Torah, he excelled as a devoted community leader, and as a munificent dispenser of charity and acts of kindness.

False Accusation

One of the students of the Talmud Torah "Etz Hayyim" used to toss coins from his hands. The principal, Rabbi Nissan Aharon Tikuchinski, asked him where he obtained the coins. The boy gave several routine-like answers: I saved them, I found them, etc.

The rabbi decided to consult the Spiritual Adviser of the Talmud Torah, Rabbi Aryeh Levin, who invited the student to his office.

Rabbi Aryeh invited the boy to sit down, and treated him with affection and warmth. He took the boy's hand in his, and told him: I have known you for a long time, and I know that you would not lie to me. Please tell me the truth. Where did you get these coins? You know that these coins have potential for harm. The whole world loves money. If you tell me the truth, all will be forgiven, as it is written, "If one confesses and ceases to do evil, he will be forgiven."

Since the rabbi had spoken to the boy so gently, caringly, and in a soft, gentle voice, his message struck a deep chord in the lad's heart, and he revealed to the rabbi that from time to time the lad would dip his hand into his father's wallet and take some coins and hide them.

When Rabbi Aryeh told the story to the father of the boy, the father fell to the floor and began to shriek in a loud voice.

Oy, oy, oy, he cried. I killed my mother-in-law! What have I done? I am a murderer!

After calming down a bit, he told this story.

From time to time some coins were missing from our house. I suspected that it was my mother-in-law, and I spoke very harshly to her. I said to my wife: We must put an end to this terrible problem. Money keeps disappearing. Our son is a righteous child; you, of course, I would never suspect. The only one left to suspect, therefore, is your mother. So now you must decide – it's either she or me! If she doesn't leave our house immediately, I am leaving the house.

My wife had no choice, so she placed her mother in a nursing home. The next day she died. Oy, oy, oy! What did I do? What terrible act did I commit? How can I face my wife now?

A huge chore lay on the shoulders of Rabbi Aryeh to calm the father. He advised him to visit the grave of his mother-in-law and ask for her forgiveness for accusing her falsely. Rabbi Aryeh promised the man that he would speak to his wife and plead with her not to bear a grudge against her husband.

Rabbi Aryeh made great efforts to counsel with the couple, and after much effort and time, succeeded in reducing the tension between them. After some months, the two were reconciled, and the matter was never brought up again.

Both Lies and Arrogance

Rabbi Raphael of Bershad loved truth and hated falsehood and arrogance. He always followed a humble path. He behaved in his home with complete simplicity. He scratched out a meager living. His forks and spoons were made of wood. His dishes were made of clay – he never owned anything made of silver or gold. At night he would sit and study by the light of a small wick in a bowl.

It happened once that one of his well-to-do Hasidim brought Rabbi Raphael's wife a gift of a menorah of silver-plated copper. When she lit candles the following Friday night, Rabbi Raphael was amazed and asked in anger: Who brought into my house something of silver that we should look like braggarts? The person who brought the gift replied: Rabbi, only the plating is silver. The candelabrum itself is only copper.

If so, said Rabbi Raphael, continuing in his anger, then this menorah is both phony and arrogant.

The person who gave the gift had to take it back.

Rabbi Raphael of Bershad
1744 – 1824

Rabbi Raphael was the most prominent of the students of Rabbi Pinhas of Koretz, who was one of the leading students of Rabbi Yisrael Baal Shem Tov.

A Child's Prayer

It happened once that Professor Abraham Joshua Heschel was present in a beautiful synagogue at the hour of prayer. He noticed that the ushers were escorting out of the synagogue a little child who had been sitting with his father, and suddenly broke out in a loud cry.

Why are you chasing that little boy? asked Professor Heschel. They replied that his cry was disturbing the prayers.

Professor Heschel answered them: To me it seems that the voice of this child, which soars through the air of this synagogue, is the only authentic sound which is heard here over all the prayers.

The Theft of the Pledge – and Its Return

It happened that a certain Jew from a small town came to Prague just before Shabbat. He had with him 10,000 dinars which he had brought to use for future purchases. He found an inn in which to lodge for the evening, but he did not want to keep his money in his pocket because that would be a violation of Shabbat law. He thus went to one of the merchants in Prague, with whom he was familiar, and asked him to hold the pouch of dinars for safe keeping until after Shabbat.

After Shabbat he went to the merchant to retrieve his money – but the merchant said to him: You never left money with me, and I have no idea what you're talking about. When the man saw that he had fallen into a trap of a swindler and a liar, he made haste to the rabbi of the city, Rabbi Yehezkel Landau.

In tears and sorrow he related the story to the rabbi. The rabbi calmed him a bit and told him to return to him the next morning. When he arrived the rabbi sent his assistant to invite the merchant from Prague, and told the guest to hide himself in the next room. He instructed him that when he hears the voice of the merchant speaking with the rabbi he should come out of his hiding place into the rabbi's office.

When the merchant came to Rabbi Yehezkel's office, the rabbi asked him for a donation of 1000 gold coins for the needs of the poor. The merchant became uncomfortable and replied: Rabbenu, in the last few years my financial situation has deteriorated, so despite my desire to contribute, I simply cannot fulfill your request.

The rabbi pressed the merchant and asked at least for hundred gold pieces. This too he refused.

Suddenly the door to the room next door opened, and the guest burst into the rabbi's office, and began to cry aloud: My master and teacher, help me! Friday afternoon I gave 10,000 dinars to the man sitting next to you, for safekeeping. And when I came last night to take back my money, he pretended that he never received a penny from me. Help me! Make him return my money!

Do you recognize this man? the rabbi asked the merchant from Prague.

Yes, I do, answered the merchant. On several occasions I entered into negotiations with him, but every time he tried to deceive me. So I stopped trading with him. Last night he suddenly came into my house and began to scream, and demand from me a pouch of money which he presumably left with me for safe-keeping. I never received anything from him.

The guest continued to scream: Thief! You yourself took the

money from my hands! And now, with such arrogance you deny it!

It seems to me, said the rabbi to the Prague merchant, that you won't end this matter unless you give him some amount of money to satisfy him.

OK, said the merchant, I will give him 100 gold pieces, on condition that he stops bothering me.

What, cried the guest? I gave him 10,000 dinarim, and now he wants to give me a pittance?! No way! He has to give me the whole amount!

Give him another 200 gold pieces, suggested the rabbi.

OK, I'll obey my rabbi, said the merchant. I'll give him 300 gold pieces, and that's it!

But the visitor did not stop screaming and crying: Unless he returns the whole 10,000 dinars, I won't leave him alone.

The rabbi continued to advise the merchant, this time suggesting that he give the traveler another 200 gold pieces. The merchant agreed. The words of the rabbis are holy in my eyes. I shall give the man 500 – as long as I will no longer have to suffer his accusations.

At that point Rabbi Yehezkel stood up and addressed the merchant: Return what you have stolen! Now it is clear to me that the visitor indeed gave you his money to keep for him during Shabbat. How do I know? Just a short while ago I asked you for a donation in this amount. But you replied to me that your financial situation would not permit it. And now suddenly you are ready to give 500 gold pieces to this stranger, since according to you, you are not obliged to give him even a penny! Thief! Return to him immediately all the money he gave you!

The merchant from Prague was overwhelmed with fear, and with tears of regret he admitted that the story of the stranger was accurate. He returned all the money to its rightful owner.

Rabbi Yehezkel Landau
1713 – 1793

Rabbi Yehezkel Landau, the Noda B'Yehudah, was among the great decisors of Jewish law in his generation. From his early youth he was considered a prodigy. When he was 21 he was already appointed as a "Dayan" (Judge) in Brody. At age 42 he was selected to hold the high office of rabbi of Prague, which he held until his death. He demonstrated exceptional leadership in a challenging and arduous period in the history of European Jewry. He was concerned for the financial welfare of the poor of his community.

He is known as the "Noda B'Yehudah" which is the title of his major work, in which he compiled his halakhic responsa. He also wrote innovative commentaries on the Talmud, and on the Shulhan Arukh, as well as collections of sermons.

A Tune and a Melody

The Power of a Niggun

Rabbi Yisrael of Modzhitz had a beautiful singing voice with which he honored God.

Let our master teach us Torah, said one of his friends. Why does he keep singing songs?

The niggun, a wordless melody, is great, answered Rabbi Yisrael, since it lifts the soul, and brings the heart of the Jewish people to their Father in heaven.

I am surprised, said one of his friends, how much effort was expended by great teachers in every generation to bring the heart of Jews to their Father in heaven. They preached in writing and orally – and they did not succeed. Is it possible that what many books of piety and ethics could not do, a song will do?

I'll give you an example, answered Rabbi Yisrael. What does all this compare to? To a miller, from the village who came to the city. He came to the window of the shop of a watchmaker, and saw among the different watches, one special one which rings so sweetly and awakens one from sleep. He went in to buy it.

Where are you from? asked the watchmaker.

From the village of so-and-so, answered the miller.

And what is your trade?

I am a miller.

And what do you want to buy?

I want to buy this watch that rings and awakens one from

sleep.

Strange, said the watchmaker, how many wheels there are in your mill, which spin and make a loud noise – and none of them succeed in awakening you. Yet this little watch, with a soft ring, how can it help you?

The way of the world, answered the miller, is that a person is not aware of something close to him. So it is with me. The huge wheels in my mill – and their loud noise – are right next to me all day and night. Thus I do not pay attention to them, and they do not awaken me from my sleep. But this little watch is new, and its soft ring will awaken me with its gentle sound.

Rabbi Yisrael concluded: It is the same in our situation. Many books of piety and ethics are close to us and do not affect us. But a melody has a freshness about it, and it has the power to arouse people and bring them back to righteousness.

Rabbi Yisrael Taub of Modzhitz
1849 – 1920

Rabbi Yisrael Taub of Modzhitz began to serve as a rabbi with the passing of his father, Rabbi Shmuel Eliyahu, in 1888. A year later he settled in Modzhitz in central Poland, where he was elected as rabbi.

He had a sweet voice and special musical talent. He composed hundreds of songs, among which was the melody for the memorial prayer in N'eilah.

His commentaries on the Torah were compiled in the book, "Divray Yisrael."

In The Old Style

It happened once that Rabbi Moshe Leib of Sassov brought a poor orphan boy and a poor orphan girl to be married under the huppah. When the huppah was spread out over the bride and groom, the rabbi's face beamed with a bright spark, since he felt in that moment a double feeling of parenthood.

He danced with great enthusiasm to the sound of melodies of the Klezmerim. He became especially excited after hearing the sweetness of one niggun – so much so that he stood up and yelled out with a full heart: I only wish that when I die they will play this niggun on the way to the cemetery.

Many years passed, and the matter was forgotten, almost...

On the fourth day of the month of Shevat, 1807, a bridal party and a troupe of Klezmerim went to a wedding in Brody. On the way they passed a cemetery and saw a large group of mourners at a funeral. They asked: Who is being buried here?

They answered: The tzaddik Rabbi Moshe Leib of Sassov.

Among the troupe of Klezmerim was an old man who had remembered what Rabbi Moshe Leib had requested many years earlier, when a certain poor couple was being married.

The elder of the musicians turned toward his friends and said: So, dear friends, play the violins, strike the drums, blow the flutes – to the tune that our rabbi loved so much!

Rabbi Shlomo Kluger of Brody
1783 – 1869

Rabbi Shlomo Kluger was one of the leading scholars in the 19th century. In his youth he served as rabbi in several communities in Poland, but most of his life he served as a Dayan (Judge) in Brody in central Galicia – which was at that time an important community of scholars.

He was a very prolific writer in all aspects of Torah. It is said that he authored some 375 books, equal to the letters of his name in Gematria (His name, Shlomo, equals 375). He devoted most of his work to responsa (answers to halakhic questions), but most of them have not been published.

Tzedakah

Contributing His Cow to the Poor

Before the tzaddik Meir of Primishlan became a rabbi to the Hasidim, he made his living from one milk cow. He would save as much money as he could to distribute it to the poor for Shabbat meals.

It happened once that he did not have even one cent to give to the poor. It occurred to him that he should slaughter his cow to distribute its meat to the poor. And so he did.

The next morning the rebbetzin went to milk the cow, and to her great surprise, she could not find it. She came to her righteous husband totally confused, and told him with a broken heart that the cow was lost.

The tzaddik replied: Heaven forbid! The cow was not lost. It went to Heaven!

Rabbi Meir of Primishlan
1780 – 1850

Rabbi Meir of Primishlan was a student of the Seer of Lublin. He became famous as a righteous folk-hero, and an amazing miracle worker. Through his Hasidic teachings he influenced masses of people. During his entire life he was concerned with the relief of the poor, and every day distributed all his money to tzedakah.

Like Rabbi Levi of Berditchev, he was an advocate for every Jew.

Most of his writings were compiled in "Or HaMeir," "Divray Meir," and "Shivhay Rabbi Meir."

The Difference Between Glass of a Window and Glass of a Mirror?

A poor Hasid who became wealthy believed that it was his wisdom that made him rich. He was full of pride, such that he did not even speak respectfully to Rabbi Michal of Zlotchov. When the wealthy Hasid walked by the home of Rabbi Michal, he pretended not even to see the rabbi, lest he be asked to contribute money to some charity.

Rabbi Michal went out to greet him, brought him into his house, and asked him to stand at the window and look outside. After a few minutes Rabbi Michal asked him: What do you see through the glass of the window?

The wealthy man replied: I see people coming and going.

Rabbi Michal then asked him to stand in front of a mirror, which he did, and then asked him: Now what do you see?

The wealthy man replied: I see myself.

Rabbi Michal said to him: What is the difference between the glass of a window, which you look through and see people – and the glass of a mirror, in which you see yourself?

Rabbi Michal answered his own question: The glass of a window has no cover of silver, so you can see other people through it. But the glass of a mirror has a covering of silver, and when you see the silver, you only see yourself.

The Poor of Your Own City Take Preference

A certain man went to visit Rabbi Aryeh Levin, and suggested that he wanted to make a contribution to the yeshivah which carries the name of Rabbi Aryeh. Rabbi Aryeh refused to accept the gift, saying that it was forbidden to him to make the contribution.

The man was amazed at this reply and asked: Why? I am a man of means!

Rabbi Aryeh replied: Your own relatives are in great need of financial help. As long as you do not help them, I am not permitted to accept your gift – since it is written: "Do not hide from your own flesh and blood," and "The poor of your own city take preference."

The wealthy man took the message to heart, and from then on he helped the members of his own family.

Why Did a Famous Rabbi Walk on the Beach?

Rabbi Avraham Hominer of Jaffa told this story: One day I went to the beach of Jaffa, and I saw a man walking with difficulty. When I came closer I saw that it was Rabbi Avraham Yitzhak Kook. I was shocked. Why would a distinguished rabbi be walking on the sands?

I walked over to him and asked, respectfully: Why is it that the honorable rabbi troubles himself to walk on the beach, and a person like me is able to drive in a car?

The rabbi was silent, but after I pressed him, he told me.

On my way I met a poor Jew who said to me: Rabbi, I am hungry. Help me!

I thought to myself – When a mitzvah comes before you, don't lose the opportunity to do it. Maybe it's a matter of life and death. So better that I should walk, and with my few pennies I can feed a hungry soul.

Fire Wood for Everyone

In all the many years that Rabbi Hayyim HaLevi Soloveitchik served as rabbi in Brisk, the congregation would supply him with all the needs of his home, including candles for lighting, and wood for burning and heating.

It happened once that the leaders of the congregation calculated and discovered that the expenses for heating the home of their rabbi were indeed very high.

They tried to figure out why the expenses were so high. They investigated and found that the room in the rabbi's house where the wood was stored was not locked, and that the poor people of the city would come and take from it as much wood as they wanted. They therefore decided to lock the storage room, and handed the key to the housekeeper.

Rabbi Hayyim found out, so he ordered that the lock be removed, so that the storage room would be open for any poor person to come and take as much as he needed.

The leaders of the congregation complained to the rabbi: Master, the fund that supplies the wood is not large enough for all the poor in the city.

If so, answered Rabbi Hayyim, let them not burn any wood in my house. I cannot sit in a house that is totally heated for me, while the poor and their families are freezing.

Rabbi Hayyim HaLevi Soloveitchik of Brisk
1853 – 1918

Rabbi Hayyim HaLevi Soloveitchik of Brisk was one of the giants of the rabbinate in Eastern Europe during the end of the 19th and beginning of the 20th century. He served as Rosh Yeshivah of Volozhin from 1880 to 1891, and as rabbi of Brisk from 1892 on. He was active in the community, but his main achievement was the development of a generation of leading scholars of Talmud and codes.

Several of his teachings were published by his students in the book "Hidushay Rabbenu Hayyim HaLevi."

Keeping a Secret

When Rabbi Yitzhak Elhanan Spector, the rabbi of Kovno, had to ask one of the wealthy leaders of Kovno for a favor for the poor, he would take the trouble to go himself to their home.

It happened once that one of the wealthy men asked the rabbi:

Why does the good rabbi take the trouble to come to me? I would gladly come to you if you would invite me to your home!

Rabbi Yitzhak Elhanan replied: I came to request a favor from you for one of the poor scholars, and I want you to do this favor for me in total sincerity. But if I would invite you to my home, you would surely think that the very fact of your coming is already half the favor.

On another occasion one of the wealthy men in town, a gentleman from a good family, suddenly became very poor. He did not want to reveal his sad situation to anyone. However, one of the businessmen of the community found out, and went to tell the matter to Rabbi Yitzhak Elhanan Spector. The two men came to an agreement to visit some of the wealthy leaders in their homes, and to request from each one a substantial contribution for this particular man, from a fine family, but without revealing the man's name.

The two of them then visited several of the larger givers in Kovno and received various contributions. But one of the very important wealthy men, who received the two of them very graciously, said to them: If the honorable rabbi himself is coming to request from me a contribution, I am prepared to give a large contribution of 25 gold coins. But I must know the name of the poor person who is of this good family – for whom the honorable rabbi himself is taking the trouble to solicit from me.

The man visiting with the rabbi hinted that for a large contribution like this, it is a good idea, perhaps, to reveal to the contributor the name of the poor person.

The rabbi refused.

Especially because of his answer, the interest of the wealthy contributor increased and he said to Rabbi Yitzhak Elhanan: My master, I am prepared to give 50 gold coins, on condition that I know the name of the recipient.

Again Rabbi Yitzhak Elhanan stood his ground, despite the suggestion of the wealthy man who came with him. Under no circumstances would he reveal the name of the poor man. Naturally the curiosity of the contributor grew even greater, and again he turned to Rabbi Yitzhak Elhanan and said: My master, I am prepared to give 100 gold coins – on condition that I know for whom I am making this contribution. And if you don't tell me, I won't give a single penny.

Again Rabbi Yitzhak Elhanan refused.

At that point the wealthy giver asked Rabbi Yitzhak Elhanan to come with him to another room where he would explain to him why he is interested in knowing the name of the poor man.

When the two of them were alone, the wealthy man began to tell the rabbi that his financial situation has suffered; his fortune is collapsing, and several times he wanted to come to the rabbi to ask his advice how to improve his situation. But he feared that for his sake he would have to reveal the information to others. Now that he sees how careful the rabbi is not to reveal the name of the person who has become impoverished, he decided to reveal to the rabbi his own difficult situation. So he is now asking, he said to the rabbi, that he be helped to find a way to get out of his deep troubles, with no one knowing anything about it.

The Reward of Mitzvot

A widowed merchant who had become very poor, had a daughter who was ready to be married. He went to Rabbi Avraham Yehoshua Heschel of Apta to consult with him about getting the necessary funds for the wedding.

The rabbi asked him how much money was required, and how much he had in hand. He replied that he needed a thousand gold pieces, but he had only one hundred.

The rabbi told him to go in peace with this advice: The first trade that comes to your attention – conclude it, and God will grant you success.

The man was puzzled. What kind of purchase can I make with this small amount of money that I have? However, he trusted the rabbi's advice, and went his way.

The merchant reached an inn, and saw merchants selling precious stones. He approached the stall where people were crowding around and looked over the diamonds that were displayed. One of the merchants asked him: Would you like to buy one of these diamonds?

Yes, he answered.

The merchant asked him how much money he had. When he replied that he had only one hundred pieces of gold, the merchant burst out laughing. Then he said to the traveler: I have a deal for you – for your one hundred pieces of gold. Buy my place in the world to come.

I agree, replied the man, on condition that you confirm the sale in writing, sealed according to custom and law.

To the laughter of those standing around, the merchant signed and sealed the document of sale, received his payment, and gave the document to the traveler. After a while the merchant sat down and began to recite chapters of the Book of Psalms.

While the merchants were sitting and laughing about this foolish traveler who paid for a place in the world to come, the wife of the merchant came by. She asked why everyone was laughing, and they told her the story. She was very shaken and told her husband: We learned in our sacred books that every Jew has a place in the world to come. Now you sold your place, and you are left stark naked of mitzvot like a pagan! I do not agree to live with a pagan like you.

The merchant began to mumble, and said that he sold it as a joke. His wife answered: I won't live with a man who does not have a place in the world to come.

The merchant turned to the traveler and said: Listen, friend, this agreement that we made was done only as a joke. Here is your money – give me back the document.

No, answered the man, a deal is a deal, I did not see it as a joke.

So let me give you a profit of several gold pieces, said the merchant – on condition that you return the document, and sell it to me.

I agree, said the man, I'll sell it for one thousand pieces of gold.

Are you crazy? cried the merchant. For some piece of paper that I gave you, you are asking a huge sum like that?

The merchant suggested that he give him one hundred gold pieces profit. The man refused.

You should know, said the traveler, that I am no bum, as you and your friends thought. I was a merchant also, but my business failed and I became poor. The holy rabbi of Apta advised me to accept the first business opportunity that came to me, since I need one thousand gold pieces for my daughter's wedding. I cannot go back on my action, even for one gold piece less than one thousand.

When the merchant realized that the man before him was very stubborn, and that all his appeals were for naught, he paid the man the required sum, and received the document in return. Immediately the merchant's wife turned to the traveler and told him that she wanted to meet the tzaddik of Apta.

My pleasure and honor, answered the man, I will bring you to him.

When they met the rabbi, she said to him: I am truly happy that I had the privilege of helping this poor man arrange the wedding for his daughter. But I have a question for you: Is the world to come really worth one thousand pieces of gold?

The rabbi replied: In the first trade, when your husband sold his place in the world to come for one hundred gold pieces, it was not worth that amount. However, in the second trade, when he redeemed his place in the world to come for one thousand gold pieces, and he helped arrange a wedding for a poor Jew, and to help him merit the mitzvah of helping a needy bride – his place in the world to come was worth far more than one thousand gold pieces.

Giving Up the World to Come to Grant Comfort

A certain woman came to Rabbi Moshe Leib of Sassov and burst out in heavy tears.

Rabbi, she cried, please pray for my daughter. She is dangerously ill!

The rabbi blessed her: May the All Merciful God send her speedy healing.

No, rabbi, she cried bitterly, I will not move from this spot until you swear on your place in the world to come that she will be healed.

I swear, answered Rabbi Moshe Leib, on my place in the world to come, that your daughter will be healed, God willing. Return home, and trust in the Healer of all flesh.

The woman left, and one of Rabbi Moshe Leib's friends asked him: My master, why did you do that? Her daughter is dangerously ill!

Rabbi Moshe Leib answered: One hour of comfort for a Jewish woman is worth the entire world to come of one Moshe Leib of Sassov.

It is Necessary to Work Hard for the World to Come

One very cold wintry night, it was snowing heavily, and Rabbi Hayyim of Tzanz was sitting and learning Torah. Suddenly he heard someone banging on his door, asking to come in.

Rabbi Hayyim rushed to the door, opened it, and in came a

Jew covered with snow, shaking like a leaf.

Rabbi Hayyim sat him near the burning fireplace, brought him a glass of wine to warm him, and then invited him to have something to eat. He then prepared a place for him to rest.

The guest apologized: Forgive me for bothering you and interrupting your studies. I was on my way to sell my wares, and have farther to travel, but outside on the road I was frozen from the cold. It was with great difficulty that I reached your home. Yours was the only home that was lit up, and now I am bothering you too much. You are even preparing a place for me to sleep – this is beneath your high honor.

Rabbi Hayyim interrupted and said: I am not preparing the bed for you, but for myself – for the world to come.

And how do I find a place for myself in the world to come? asked the visitor. In this world I find almost no enjoyment. My whole life is devoted to my work. I have no rest. Can I hope at least that I will have a place in the world to come?

Rabbi Hayyim sighed and answered: If you don't enjoy this world, where you work so much, how do you expect to find a place in the world to come? If you don't work for enjoyment now, you surely won't have time to work for a place in the world to come!

The Power of a Mitzvah

Two exceptionally righteous brothers, students of the Gaon of Vilna, were Rabbi Moshe Ashkenazi and Rabbi Yitzhak, author of "Brit Olam" on the wisdom of the Kabbalah.

All year long Rabbi Moshe would wander in the villages and

teach Torah, delve unobtrusively into his studies and in his prayers. He would return home for the major Festivals (Pesah, Shavuot, Sukkot) when he had earned enough money to feed his family.

Just as it was the custom of the previous generation of Hasidim to cling to one special mitzvah – and be totally committed to it – he too was devoted especially to the mitzvah of "tzitzit" (ritual fringes attached to a four-cornered garment). His custom was not to move even a few feet without wearing his tzitzit.

It happened once that his holy brother, Rabbi Yitzhak, became ill, and the doctors decided that his case was hopeless. They immediately sent for Rabbi Moshe who was traveling in various villages, so that he would pray for mercy for his brother.

Rabbi Moshe came to his brother's bed, and asked everyone to leave the room. When the two brothers remained alone, Rabbi Moshe took off his tzitzit, placed them on his brother's bed and said: "Master of the Universe, I have been very strict about one mitzvah with all my heart, and that is the mitzvah of wearing tzitzit.

I am now prepared to forgo all my reward in the world to come for performing this mitzvah so carefully – on condition that the merit of my doing this mitzvah shall be transferred to my sick brother, so that he will be cured of his illness.

The tzaddik Rabbi Yitzhak was cured of his illness by virtue of his brother's prayer, and he lived another fifteen years.